THE CHRIST-CENTERED LIFE

31 DISCIPLESHIP LETTERS EXPLAINING HOW THE GOSPEL SHAPES FOUNDATIONAL CHRISTIAN PRACTICES, VALUES, AND BELIEFS TO BE CENTERED IN CHRIST

by
Daniel Slott
Foreword by Chuck Lawless

The Christ-Centered Life:
31 Discipleship Letters Explaining How the Gospel Shapes Foundational
Christian Practices, Values, and Beliefs to Be Centered in Christ

ISBN: 978-0692908242

Printed in the United States of America

To my daughter, Penelope.

Although you are too young to understand these things now, my hope and prayer is that one day you will find your heart in joyful agreement with the apostle Paul when he said, "Indeed, I count everything as loss because of the surpassing worth of knowing Christ Jesus my Lord" (Philippians 3:8).

CONTENTS

Part 3: Foundational Christian Beliefs

Part 4: Go and Make Disciples

Part 5: Extra Resources

ENDORSEMENTS

Something I most appreciate about *The Christ-Centered Life* is that it is the product of a missionary-heart, grappling with how to grow up young believers in a setting far from Western Christianity. At the same time, it continually directs the disciple to God's Word as the source for truth, including the truth about suffering for Christ and spiritual endurance.

    –**Randy Adams**, Executive Director, Northwest Baptist Convention, Vancouver, WA

The Great Commission commands us to make disciples, not decisions. *The Christ-Centered Life* is a wonderful resource for the discipleship process. This work is rooted in Scripture, focused on Christ, and grounded in the gospel. The "Personal Reflections" sections encourage life application versus mere head knowledge. I highly commend this outstanding resource for your discipleship ministry.

    –**Timothy K. Beougher**, Associate Dean, Billy Graham School of Missions, Evangelism and Ministry; Professor of Evangelism and Church Growth, The Southern Baptist Theological Seminary, Louisville, KY

This book is a valuable resource for the believer and those being discipled in the church. It is readable and simple, yet comprehensive and practical. *The Christ-Centered Life* leads a believer to marinate in the joyous gospel truths, then teaches them to actively and faithfully participate in the Great Commission as Christ commanded.

–**Hannah Carter**, Certified Counselor with the Association of Certified Biblical Counselors, Louisville, KY; Counselor, One-Eighty Counseling and Education, Louisville, KY

The Christ-Centered Life is a fantastic journey into being a disciple and the process of making disciples. I highly recommend this as a valuable resource in our fulfilling the Great Commission.

–**Aaron Harvie,** Senior Pastor, Highview Baptist Church, Louisville, KY

I want to highly recommend *The Christ-Centered Life* by Daniel Slott. I have known Daniel for a number of years and find him to be a man who loves the church! That love is made evident in this book. It is simple and practical, yet profound, as he thinks through what the new believer needs to know to begin his or her journey in the faith.

–**John Klaassen,** Associate Professor and Program Coordinator of Global Studies, Boyce College, Louisville, KY; Doctor of Missiology Program Director, The Southern Baptist Theological Seminary, Louisville, KY

The great work of the Christian ministry is to bring sinners to life in Christ, and then to encourage and enable them to become fully like Christ. This task is called "disciple-making." The task is neither easy nor quick. *The Christ-Centered Life* offers a solidly biblical and useful approach for enabling believers to "grow up in every way into him who is the head, into Christ" (Ephesians 4:15).

> –**George H. Martin,** Professor of Christian Missions and World Religions, The Southern Baptist Theological Seminary, Louisville, KY; Editor, Southern Baptist Journal of Missions and Evangelism

You do not need to be in a church leadership position for very long before you are asked the question, "Can you recommend any good resources for discipleship or for how to live the Christian life?" There are, of course, many resources available. But one I will be sure to recommend is *The Christ-Centered Life*. This resource presents thirty-one lessons on the Christian life and does so in letter format, much like the letters of the New Testament. There are three main reasons why I like this resource. First, I like the author's approach. In the Preface, he makes this statement: "Discipleship ... requires personal relationships and structure." Those two phrases—personal relationships and structure—are essential to any type of successful discipleship program. Their incorporation here assures that this book is based on a foundation that will work. Second, I like the content. A look through the Table of Contents indicates the three major foundations that will be presented here: Christian Practices, Christian Values, and Christian Beliefs. In short, the author includes topics on how to live the Christian life, what are the qualities that should characterize Christians, and what are the basic biblical beliefs that a Christian ought to have. As I think through what ought to be included in a discipleship work, this resource has them all. Third, I like the amount of Scripture that is included in each of the thirty-one letters. Discipleship principles are good, but not if they can't be tied in and related to what the Bible teaches. This book is saturated with the Word of God. Those who will take the time to look up the Scriptures that are referenced will have a much deeper appreciation for what the Bible teaches and how it speaks to our past, present, and future in our walk with God and with others. Daniel Slott has done the church a valuable service by producing this work. Hopefully, many Christians will use this common-sense approach to knowing and growing in the Word of God.

–**David DeKlavon,** Associate Dean for Academic Administration, Associate Professor of New Testament Interpretation, Boyce College, Louisville, KY

FOREWORD

As a young believer in the 1970s, I knew little about the Word of God. My church taught the Word every Sunday in Sunday school classes and the worship services, for which I am deeply grateful today. They helped me to build a gospel foundation, but I wish someone had put his arm around me and helped me to walk better in obedience and faith. I would have devoured letters like these you find in this resource.

Daniel Slott, the author of these letters, has a heart for nonbelievers, whether they are our neighbors or the nations around the world. His Great Commission passion that you will find in this study is genuine; it's deeply seated and firmly held.

His passion, though, is a *complete* Great Commission passion; that is, he understands that reaching people for Christ is only one step in the process. It's not enough to guide people to faith in Jesus—we must also help them begin to grow in that relationship. We must walk beside believers, grounding them in the Word and helping them to obey everything Jesus commanded.

To *not* do so is risky indeed. We need only look around in many North American churches to see the results of negligent or nonexistent discipleship strategies. Believers struggle to find victory. Their commitment to spiritual disciplines is sporadic at best. The enemy that prowls about (1 Peter 5:8) wins far too often. The church looks like the world, and the world ignores the gospel message.

Written in a conversational letter style, this series of discipleship letters seeks to fill the discipleship void for new and older believers alike. Christ is its center. The gospel is its message. Obedience is its application. You will be a stronger believer because you have eavesdropped on this conversation.

Chuck Lawless

Wake Forest, NC

PREFACE

The Great Commission is simple: make disciples. So how's that going? If you are like me, you have found that is no easy task. Sure, I've had seasons where it's been great, as I'm sure you have as well. And I'm sure I've made every mistake imaginable, and might I say *unimaginable*, on my quest to learn myself and teach others to follow Christ. And each time, even in my failures, God has provided gracious comfort that He is firmly in control. But if there is one thing I've learned along the way, it is that I need help. And I'm guessing you wouldn't be reading this book if you didn't feel the same way.

I often wonder if I am defining discipleship the same way Jesus would have when He called a few fishermen to follow Him or as He explained to the Twelve the cost of following Him as the crowds deserted Him because the teaching was too difficult (John 6:67). I wonder what the disciples must have thought as Jesus described the cost of true discipleship in Luke 9. I think it's a healthy exercise for the mind and fruitful for the soul. But even while I may never fully grasp what Jesus meant, one thing is for certain: discipleship is a call to die to self and live fully for Jesus Christ. It is a commitment that begins with personal devotion to live for Christ and is fully expressed also in a commitment to help another do the same.

Discipleship was meant to be life-on-life, not a rigid curriculum. It requires personal relationships and structure. Relationships allow the flexibility to go where the conversation will naturally go, while structure takes the conversation where it is sometimes uncomfortable to go. Striking a balance between these two important elements will keep the discipleship personal, relational, and intentional. Most believers understand they have a God-given responsibility to make disciples and are willing to do so, but they do not know how to get started or where to go.

The goal for some believers is to use only the Bible to disciple another. But that is an unrealistic expectation for most believers today. It sounds great, but is improbable for most. It's not unrealistic to expect it long-term, but it is when a person is first learning to disciple another. As members in our respective local churches, we have a decision to make. We either want all believers to participate in the ministry of discipleship in the local church, or we will continue to expect pastors to solely fill this important responsibility—or worse yet, no one at all. The ministry of the church was never meant to be fulfilled by a handful of people, nor were the nations meant to be discipled by a select few. Yet this is the hard truth for most churches today. If we truly want to see every member equipped to make disciples, we need tools everyone can use. And that is my intention for this work: to help you, the believer, love and obey Jesus more, and to help you, the disciple-maker, participate in the God-given command to make disciples, starting where you have been sovereignly placed.

The purpose of The Christ-Centered Life is to start the conversation, guide the conversation, ground the conversation in Scripture, and catapult the conversation from general biblical principles into personal, practical, and gospel-centered application. My hope and prayer is that this book will be a helpful resource for you and your church, helping you equip yourself and others to joyfully and faithfully participate in the Great

Commission to go and make disciples of all nations, baptizing them in the name of the Father and of the Son and of the Holy Spirit, teaching them to obey all that Christ commanded, while remembering the promise of our Lord Jesus, "Behold, I am with you always, to the end of the age" (Matthew 28:20).

INTRODUCTION:
A LIFE CENTERED IN CHRIST

A few years ago, my wife and I helped plant a church in East Asia. As foreign missionaries, we were limited in what we could do. For example, we could not attend the corporate worship service on Sundays or attend community groups throughout the week. We helped from the shadows, and it was our joy and honor to do whatever we could to help this young church. One of the ways we did this was by helping them develop a discipleship strategy that everyone could use. Working in conjunction with East Asian pastors, I wrote a discipleship guide that explains how the gospel shapes foundational Christian practices, values, and beliefs to be centered in Christ. As I sought the Lord's leading and worked tirelessly with national pastors to develop this important tool, I sensed the Lord convicting me to allow seven "anchors" to guide this project. Those seven anchors are as follows:

Anchor One: *The Christ-Centered Life* Makes Christ the Center

The focus of any discipleship book should be undeniably Christ-centered. Discipleship is the process of learning to turn all things in life to point to Christ (Luke 9:23). It is the lifelong process of learning to allow the gospel to shape everything in our lives to be centered in Christ. Our thoughts, affections, and actions all point to something–either a self-centered motive or Christ. Christ-centered discipleship is the process of learning to analyze every thought, feeling, and action in light of Christ and trusting God's Spirit to change that life to be like Christ as we depend on God's daily grace with the same tenacity, humility, and dependency we trusted God with at conversion. The Christ-centered life is motivated by a love for Christ, obedient to the commands of Christ, modeled after the life of Christ, humbled by the sacrifice of Christ, confident in the return of Christ, and empowered by the Spirit of Christ. It is the life that makes Jesus the source of strength, object of affection, and ultimate prize, both during the journey and at the end. The purpose of this book is to show how Christ is the center of everything in the lives of believers and everything flows from our relationship with Him.

Anchor Two: *The Christ-Centered Life* Explains How the Gospel Shapes All Things

The gospel reveals how God intervened for us as nonbelievers to do what we could not–give us peace with Him. In the same way, the gospel reveals how God intervenes for us now as believers to do what we cannot–conform us to the image of Christ (Romans 8:29). The gospel is not only the power of our salvation in Christ, but also the power of our spiritual growth in Christ. The gospel should inspire, define, and shape all things to be centered in Christ. This happens in many ways. God's Spirit shapes our minds, hearts, and actions when we learn to see the world through the lens of the gospel (Romans 12:2). For example, the gospel explains how we are to understand God as Creator and holy. The gospel reveals how we are to understand the heart of God, a heart that hates sin and loves what is good. The gospel instructs us to approach God's throne with confidence that His mercy covers our failures (Hebrews 4:16). The gospel defines who we are in Christ (2 Corinthians 5:17). And it is the gospel that provides us with the perfect example to follow: Jesus. The more we learn to embrace, share, and live out the truth of the gospel, the more we are able to think, feel, and act like Jesus, which is what I mean by being centered in Christ. That is the transforming power of the gospel, and through the empowerment of the Holy Spirit, you and I participate in this process by bringing our hearts, souls, minds, and strengths into alignment with God's will by allowing the gospel to shape every area of our lives to be centered in Christ.

Anchor Three: *The Christ-Centered Life* Addresses the Head, Heart, and Hands of Discipleship

If God's plan is to conform us into the image of Christ, then we will need radical change in three areas: our minds (beliefs), hearts (values), and actions (practices). If not careful, though, discipleship methods can easily favor one dimension over the others. Striking a balance is necessary for healthy Christ-centered growth. God's Spirit is actively working in us now to renew our minds so that we think the way Christ would think (Romans 12:2). In the same way, the Spirit of God is actively working in our hearts by reshaping our emotions and affections. As our minds and hearts are molded by the truth of the gospel, this internal transformation will be demonstrated in our outward actions. The goal in this is to conform us into the image of Christ so we begin to think, feel, and act like Christ. This can be a slow process, but over time we will find we are able to honor God with our minds (firmly believe the promises of God and confidently pray to Him), our hearts (affectionately love Him and passionately worship Him), and our actions (joyfully obey His commands and pursue a life of holiness). I will explain these things further in my letters, but it is important to understand two things: Only God can change your life, and He expects you to actively participate in the process through the empowerment of the Holy Spirit in you. This is called discipleship.

Anchor Four: *The Christ-Centered Life* Can Be Used by Anyone

One of my goals for this book was to keep it simple and easily reproducible so everyone, from the elders of the church to the youngest of believers, can participate in the discipleship of another. It's written in the form of short letters from the perspective of a missionary church planter (myself) to members of a local church. Letters are historically how church leaders have encouraged others in the faith and explained how to obey all the commands of Christ. By explaining biblical topics with clear teaching and simple definitions, it is meant to bring people together to discuss how these things apply in everyday life. And by providing self-reflection questions after each letter, it also makes personal discussion convenient and relevant. Discipleship cannot happen in isolation. Discipleship is two fold; it is learning to turn everything in life toward Christ and helping another do the same. The truth is you're not obeying everything Christ commanded unless you are reproducing yourself by making more disciples. This book is meant to help you cultivate a Christ-centered discipleship community, one-on-one or in a small group setting, by creating a forum to discuss the practical application of the gospel in everyday life.

Anchor Five: *The Christ-Centered Life* Covers the Basics of the Christian Faith

In ministry today, it's not uncommon to hear the phrase "get back to the basics," but it's not always clear what that means. This work is my interpretation of what the basics are: the thirty-one basic topics, including the most pertinent content for understanding those topics, that every believer should know, embrace, and apply. The first ten letters are basic practices every believer should be actively involved in. The next ten letters are common values every believer should hold. The following ten letters are beliefs every believer should understand. And the thirty-first letter is the call to go and make disciples. With each letter being three to five short paragraphs, my goal is to provide the irreducible minimum for each topic to keep it concise and relevant.

Anchor Six: *The Christ-Centered Life* Provides Deep Theology in Small Doses

The writer of Hebrews urges his audience to move past elementary teachings and on to maturity (Hebrews 6:1). In the previous chapter he compares this to milk and solid food. In East Asia one of the things you hear most often about the church leaders is their requests for theological education. We hear this in the West and rush to provide it. But what many Western leaders have found is that although these East Asian leaders are eager to feast on deep theological teaching, they don't have the spiritual maturity to fully process what they are getting. Why? Because more than a formal theological training issue in East Asia, there is a discipleship issue first. And it's the same in the West. There are portions of this writing that deal with deep theological concepts. We shouldn't be afraid to chew on such things. Milk is necessary for proper nourishment, but it is a means to an end. We are meant to move beyond milk and enjoy the richness of solid food (Hebrews 5:14).

Anchor Seven: *The Christ-Centered Life* Contrasts the World's View with the Christian's

One of the great responsibilities we have to help a new believer understand what it means to be a follower of Christ is to help that person discern how the world's definition of everyday values differs significantly from the Bible. Our values govern and shape our thoughts and actions, and often times without our conscious approval. That is why it is important to explain how we as believers define these terms differently from the world by comparing them side-by-side. As believers we need to be ready to not only give a defense for our faith but also to share how we define our values from a biblical perspective. Take, for example, the words *faith*, *hope*, and *joy*. These are common words in every believer's vocabulary but are difficult to define. This book seeks to do just that by allowing Scripture to interpret Scripture.

The Christ-Centered Life Meets You Where You Are and Provides a Path to Move Forward

Although originally written for a local church in East Asia, this resource can be helpful for all believers from all cultures and backgrounds because it is based on solid biblical principles. Discipleship is sometimes intimidating, but it does not have to be difficult. My challenge to you would be this: make a plan today to move toward being a disciple-maker. You may be young in the faith and, for this season, it may be beneficial to invite a more mature believer to walk alongside of you as you learn to follow Christ. That's a great thing. Or you may be mature in the faith and convicted it is time to step out and become a maker of disciples. That's great, too. Regardless of where you are today, my hope is that this book can help. For the process to work, each person needs to be committed to reading one letter on a routine basis (I recommend one a week), look up the verses referenced in that letter, answer the self-reflection questions honestly, and meet with a discipleship partner to discuss your responses. Start each meeting by discussing what you have learned in your daily devotions and with accountability from the week before. You can use a question like, "Describe how you practically applied what we talked about last time" to ensure each participant is internalizing and acting on what he or she is learning. And to help you evaluate the meeting once it is over, I've included eight questions in the back of the book under "Extra Resources." These are not questions to discuss during the meeting, but are questions to evaluate whether or not the conversation stayed on topic. With thirty-one letters, meeting weekly will take approximately six months to work through the book. This simple process fosters incredible opportunities to discuss how the gospel applies in everyday life. Lastly, although this material can be used in a variety of formats, I strongly suggest discipleship being rooted in and through a local church. This does not mean discipleship meetings should take place in a church building, although they can. Location is not the issue. Rather, I'm suggesting church members rally around other church members in personal conversations so that a discipleship culture is cultivated and a DNA for multiplying disciples is created. Furthermore, only discipleship in a local church will allow young and old believers alike to fully experience the body of Christ fulfilling her age-old calling.

Never Stop Pursuing Your Joy in Christ

I want to end this introduction by reminding you of the depth of God. I hope these letters help you understand spiritual concepts that can be difficult to comprehend, but there will still be things you do not understand, especially your first time reading them. That is alright; the wisdom of God is higher than man's. But those moments should lead you to a place of awe and wonder at the depth of God's glory (Romans 11:33). Ephesians 2:4–7 describes God's riches as immeasurable. Eternity is not long enough to fully measure the wisdom, love, mercy, power, beauty, and strength of God.[1] This is great news, because nothing will ever be too much for God. There is no question that will confuse Him, no problem He cannot overcome, and no sorrow He cannot comfort. It is why heaven will never be boring and why the Christian life will never be mundane. Jesus is the eternal fountain that never runs dry and the bread that never goes stale.

My hope in writing these letters is that your knowledge of God would be ever expanding and your desire to proclaim His name among the nations would be ever-growing; but most importantly, I hope your love for Christ and joy in His salvation would be ever-increasing. Never stop digging, desiring, thirsting, or pressing to know Christ more, for there is no end to the depths of God. Even when the Lord feels far away from you, never stop eagerly expecting to hear from Him. And never stop applying, reflecting, and depending on God's daily grace while you pursue your greatest delight in Him. In fact, that is what my first letter to you is all about. God bless you, and may you not forget the promise of Jesus in Matthew 28:20 when He said, "I am with you always, to the end of the age."

To the praise of His glory,

Daniel Slott

March 2016

PART 1

FOUNDATIONAL CHRISTIAN PRACTICES

1

GLORIFY GOD

So, whether you eat or drink, or whatever
you do, do all to the glory of God.
1 CORINTHIANS 10:31

I hope this letter finds you doing well and walking in the grace that is yours in Christ and that my introduction helped explain how the gospel shapes all things to be centered in Christ. In my first letter, I want to explain the glory of God and how you can glorify Him by pursuing your joy in Jesus.

Christ Restored Your Ability to Glorify God

When Christ reconciled you to God, He also restored your ability to live according to God's original design—to glorify God. The "glory of God" is a term used to describe the magnificent, infinite worth, beauty, and power of God. To glorify God means to honor God by directing your affection, allegiance, attention, and praise toward Him. It means you put the interest of God above the interest of your self. It would be like saying, "Instead of a self-centered life, I want to live a God-centered life." This will affect how you make decisions, treat others, and spend your time, even when nobody is watching. Your example to glorify God was set by Jesus, who glorified God in every way (John 17:1–5).

God's Glory Is Displayed throughout History

Revelation 4:11 says God is worthy to receive all glory, honor, and power because by His will everything was created. The psalmist said, "The heavens declare the glory of God" (19:1) and that you should "ascribe to the Lord the glory due His name" (29:2). The prophet Isaiah declares the whole earth is full of His glory (6:3), people are created for His glory (43:7), and that He will not give His glory to another (48:11). In 2 Corinthians 4:4–6, Paul described the gospel as the glory of Christ and Jesus as the image of God. The gospel is the glory of Jesus who is the radiance of the glory of God (Hebrews 1:3). Ephesians 1:3–14 says God redeemed you and brought you into fellowship with Himself to the praise of His glory. Philippians 2:11 says that every tongue will confess Jesus is Lord, to the glory of God. You were created for the glory of God and redeemed for the glory of God the Father, and as a follower of Christ you are to now live for the glory of God (1 Corinthians 10:31). You honor God and reflect His glory by living with one single passion—to the praise of God's glory.

God Will Be Most Glorified in Your Life
When You Desire Him above All

God does not want cold-hearted, ritualistic followers. Jesus said the Pharisees honored Him with their lips, but their hearts were far from Him (Matthew 15:8). God will be most glorified in your life when you desire Him above all else. In Deuteronomy 4, Moses told the Israelite people to watch closely lest they forget the covenant of God. In verse 24 he said, "For the Lord your God is a consuming fire, a jealous God." It is difficult to accept the idea that God is a jealous God. How could the God of the universe be jealous of anything? It is difficult to understand because you are human, but God is divine. He is the perfectly holy Creator. When God called for the Israelites' complete devotion, He was drawing them to the only thing that could satisfy their souls—Himself.[2] The same is true for you. Demanding your praise, honor, and allegiance is the most loving thing He can do. Not only will your heart be most glad when you draw near to Him and pursue your satisfaction in Him, but it is the best display of His glory. There is no contradiction between glorifying God and pursuing your joy in Him (John 15:11).

God's Glory Shines Brightest When Your Joy Abounds

Retired pastor John Piper succinctly summarizes this truth by expressing "God is most glorified in us, when we are most satisfied in Him."[3] Jesus told two parables to help explain this. In Matthew 13:44, Jesus said the kingdom of heaven is like a man who discovered a treasure hidden in a field. The man joyfully sold all he had to buy the field. When

God is your greatest treasure, you will rejoice in Him above everything else. In Matthew 13:45–46, Jesus said the kingdom of heaven is like a pearl collector who sold all he had to buy a pearl of great worth. When God becomes more valuable to you than anything else, then you accurately reflect His infinitely glorious worth. It explains why God invites His people to delight in Him (Isaiah 55:1–2), why Habakkuk could still rejoice when he had nothing (Habakkuk 3:17–19), why Paul considered everything as trash compared to the "surpassing worth of knowing Jesus" (Philippians 3:8), why the psalmist said, "In your presence there is fullness of joy, at your right hand are pleasures forevermore" (Psalm 16:11), and why Paul's chief concern, whether by life or death, was for Christ to be honored (Philippians 1:20). When Jesus is your greatest treasure, God's glory shines brightest.

I hope this letter helped explain the glory of God and how you can glorify God by pursuing your joy in Jesus. My next letter will teach you what it means to trust the gospel every day and explain why trust is the foundation of obedience.

PERSONAL REFLECTIONS

In your own words, summarize what you have learned in this letter and describe how it applies to your life.

God wants to be glorified in me because He made for that Reason. He is most glorified when I am satisfied in Him.

How does the gospel shape your ability to glorify God?

The Gospel is the message of restoration, through Jesus I am able to glorify God.

What does it mean to glorify God?

To Exalt Him, Honor Him, give Him what is owed.

How did Christ restore your ability to glorify God?

Paying for Sin on Cross

Why is God most glorified when your joy abounds in Christ?

'Cause we are living according to God's purpose for our lives.

What is your daily plan to glorify God this week?

What other questions do you have?

2

TRUST THE GOSPEL

Now I would remind you, brothers, of the gospel I preached
to you, which you received, in which you stand, and by
which you are being saved, if you hold fast to the word
I preached to you—unless you believed in vain.
1 CORINTHIANS 15:1-2

I hope this letter finds you doing well and walking in the joy that is yours in Christ and that my last letter helped explain how to glorify God by delighting in Christ. In this letter, I will teach you what it means to trust the gospel every day and explain why trust is the foundation of obedience.

Remember the Gospel

In 1 Corinthians 15:1-11, the apostle Paul, one of the writers of the New Testament, not only reminded the church of the gospel, but he also charged them to continue to trust the gospel daily by calling them to stand in it. The gospel is the story of God's plan to reconcile sinners to

Himself through the life, death, and resurrection of Christ, and transform them into the image of Christ. By standing in the gospel, Paul was calling believers to firmly believe the promises of God, so as not to retreat or believe anything that contradicts the gospel (Romans 5:2; Galatians 5:1; Philippians 4:1). The same is true for you today. Trusting God has a past, present, and future dimension to it. The past tense of trusting Christ is believing that He has already reconciled you to God. The present tense is trusting that God's Spirit is actively working in and through you in this very moment. The future tense of trusting Christ is believing that Christ will fulfill all His promises. When Paul called believers to stand in the gospel, he was not calling them to trust God only on the first day they believed, but every day after that as well.

All Things Work Together for Good

We live in a fallen world that sometimes makes it difficult to believe the promises of God. But we have to believe one simple truth about God: God sovereignly ordains everything that will happen for His glory and your good. Do you remember in my last letter I explained how glorifying God and delighting in Jesus were inseparably connected? It is the same here. Everything God does magnifies His glory, and it is also the best possible outcome for you, if your greatest treasure is God.

Romans 8:28 says, "And we know that for those who love God all things work together for good, for those who are called according to His purpose." This means if you are to stand strong and trust the gospel every day, you have to believe that everything that happens, good or difficult, happens for a reason. It is trusting that God will use every circumstance to draw His people to Him. When life is great, God's people rejoice in Him. And when life is difficult, God's people find refuge in Him. God uses the difficult times in life to draw His people closer to Him, and it will be the same for you.

For example, you will have times when friends, family, and coworkers will try to discourage you in your faith. When that happens, respond in grace just as Jesus did when He was crucified, and remember two things. First, they have the same spiritual blindness you had before God intervened and opened your eyes through hearing the gospel (2 Corinthians 4:3–6). Share the gospel with them, and ask God to open their eyes to their need for Him. Second, trust that God has a plan, and He is allowing that circumstance to happen for your good. To keep trusting the gospel means you trust God is working in all things for your good and for His glory.

Obedience Requires Love and Trust

The Great Commission (Matthew 28:18–20) instructs me to teach you how to obey all the commands of Christ. Learning to trust God is the first step in obedience. In order to faithfully obey God's commands, you have to believe He has your best interest in mind, and you have to be motivated by your love for Him. In my letter on Christ-Centered Love, I'll explain this further. But know this: God wants you to obey Him out of a heart that loves and trusts Him. When you love and trust God, obedience will naturally follow. Love brings obedience; cold-hearted obedience never produces love. God does not command your obedience because He needs anything, and He is not honored through empty rituals. Obedience is an act of worship. When you obey God, you are saying in your heart, "God, I trust Your way is better than whatever temporary satisfaction disobeying might bring."

Trusting God will be a lifelong journey. As you enter each new stage of life, you will need to learn how to trust God in that stage. Ask Him to help you trust His promises by strengthening your faith and to fill your heart with joyful obedience.

I hope this letter helped explain what it means to trust the gospel every day and why trust is the foundation of obedience. My next letter will explain how to develop a vibrant daily relationship with Christ by abiding in Him.

PERSONAL REFLECTIONS

In your own words, summarize what you have learned in this letter and describe how it applies to your life.

_____

_____

_____

_____

How does the gospel shape your ability and desire to trust God's promises and obey His commands?

_____

_____

_____

_____

What is the gospel?

_____

_____

_____

_____

What does it mean to trust the gospel daily as a believer?

_____

_____

_____

_____

Why does obedience require love and trust?

_____

_____

_____

_____

What is your daily plan to trust the promises of God this week?

_____

_____

_____

_____

What other questions do you have?

_____

_____

_____

_____

3

ABIDE IN CHRIST

I am the vine; you are the branches. Whoever abides
in me and I in him, he it is that bears much fruit,
for apart from me you can do nothing.
JOHN 15:5

I hope this letter finds you doing well and walking in the confidence that is yours in Christ and that my last letter helped explain how to trust the gospel every day. In this letter, I want to teach you how to develop a vibrant daily relationship with Jesus by abiding in Him.

Jesus Is Your Source of Life, Power, and Growth

As the time of Jesus' earthly ministry was coming to an end and the cross was quickly approaching, He gathered His disciples together and used a metaphor of a vine and branches to teach them an important truth. A *metaphor* is a literary term that is used to teach a spiritual truth. Although metaphors can be complicated to understand, they help explain deep spiritual meanings. In John 15:1–11, Jesus used the metaphor of a vine and branches to teach three things: Jesus as the vine is your only source of life, power, and growth (vv. 1, 4, 5); God the Father as the vinedresser will sometimes use difficult circumstances to help you be more fruitful (vv. 1, 2, 6, 8); Jesus wants you to bear fruit (vv. 2, 4, 5, 8, 16).

Spiritual Fruit Is Internal and External

The "fruit" in the metaphor is a spiritual fruit that has both an internal and external dimension. Look at the list provided in Galatians 5:22–23. These fruits are from God and reflect the character of God. When you abide in Christ, they will be reflected in your mind, heart, and actions. Bearing fruit is a testimony of how God is working in and through you to accomplish His will for your life and those around you.

The Vinedresser Removes and Prunes Branches

It is important to understand the two primary purposes of the vinedresser. First, the vinedresser removes branches that do not bear fruit. The point Jesus is making is that branches that do not bear fruit were never truly believers, because true believers will bear fruit—Jesus as the Vine and the Father as the Vinedresser make sure they do. This is not teaching believers can lose their salvation or that God will give up on you. Jesus makes it abundantly clear throughout the book of John that believers cannot be taken from Him. For example, in John 10:29, Jesus said God is greater than all, and no one is able to snatch you out of His hand.

Second, Jesus was also teaching that the Father uses every circumstance to accomplish His will. God desires for His children to bear fruit, and pruning is for the purpose of bearing more fruit. Sometimes God will allow difficult things to happen so that He can use the circumstance to build character and hope in you, which transforms you more and more into the image of Jesus (Romans 5:4). God is sovereign and reigns over all. Anything that happens, no matter how bad it might seem, is ultimately for your good. Even in times of great sorrow, the Lord will be working through that to bear fruit of hope and joy.

Develop a Vibrant Daily Relationship with Jesus by Abiding in Him

In John 15:7–11, Jesus told His disciples to abide in Him. When you abide in Christ your prayers are answered (15:7), God is glorified through the bearing of fruit (15:8), and your joy is full (15:11). So what does it mean to abide in Christ? It means to be a disciple of Christ. John said you prove to be Christ's disciple by continuing in His Word (John 15:8), loving one another (13:34–35), and bearing much fruit (15:8). In 1 John, he said to abide in Christ means to walk in the same way that Christ walked (2:6) and that "no one who abides in Him keeps on sinning" (3:6). In other words, to abide in something means you continue in that thing. To abide in Jesus is to continue trusting, hoping, loving, obeying, depending, and rejoicing in Him daily. It means you have a growing, vibrant daily relationship with Jesus. To abide in Christ also means His Word abides in you. This is more than a commitment to daily Bible reading. It is a commitment to allow God's Word to shape how you think, feel, and act. It requires a teachable spirit that approaches God's Word with eager expectation to hear from God and be transformed from the inside out. It's an authentic desire to know, love, and serve God better. Abiding in Christ means starting every day with a renewed passion to trust, follow, and be used by Him.

I hope this letter helped explain how to develop a vibrant daily relationship with Jesus by abiding in Him. My next letter will explain what it means to grow more and more into the image of Christ. This is called *sanctification.*

PERSONAL REFLECTIONS

In your own words, summarize what you have learned in this letter and describe how it applies to your life.

_____

_____

_____

_____

How does the gospel shape your ability to abide in Christ?

_____

_____

_____

_____

What does it mean to abide in Jesus?

_____

_____

_____

_____

How does God use difficult circumstances to bear fruit in you?

_____

_____

_____

_____

What does it mean to allow God's Word to abide in you?

_____

_____

_____

_____

What is your daily plan to abide in Christ this week?

_____

_____

_____

_____

What other questions do you have?

_____

_____

_____

_____

4

GROW IN CHRISTLIKENESS

And we know that for those who love God all things work
together for good, for those who are called according to His
purpose. For those whom He foreknew He also predestined
to be conformed to the image of His Son in order that
He might be the firstborn among many brothers.

ROMANS 8:28-29

I hope this letter finds you doing well and walking in the strength that is yours in Christ and that my last letter helped explain how to abide in Christ and experience His complete joy in your heart. In this letter, I will teach you how to conform to the image of Christ in a way that is honoring to God and reflective of the gospel. We call this process *sanctification*.

Conform to the Image of the Son

1 Thessalonians 4:3 tells you what God's will is for your life: your sanctification. Sanctification is the process, beginning at conversion, by which

you are enabled to progressively become more like Christ through the presence and power of the indwelling Holy Spirit. It is the process of your mind, heart, and actions being conformed more and more to the mind, heart, and actions of Christ. Sanctification is easy to talk about, yet difficult to do. It requires you to view struggles through the lens of Scripture, take personal responsibility for your sins, pursue change through Christ-centered application, and actively participate in spiritual growth through the empowerment of the Holy Spirit (Romans 8:13; 1 Timothy 4:7–8). Sanctification will teach you to focus on heart issues so that through inward transformation, outward transformation will result.

Sanctification Has an "Already" and "Not Yet" Implication

The Bible speaks of sanctification in two forms: definitive and progressive. The definitive form is exemplified in 1 Corinthians 1:2, that says we were sanctified by the blood of Christ at conversion. The progressive sense is exemplified in 2 Corinthians 3:18 by demonstrating the continual process of growth. The sanctification process is a cycle of sin, repentance, renewal, and growth. The goal of sanctification is not modifying external behavior, but rather, identifying heart issues that are the source of external behavior and applying the gospel to help you be more like Christ. While your desire for sin will become progressively weakened, you will not experience complete victory over sin until heaven. First John 1:8 teaches every believer still has sin. Sanctification is a process, not a destination.

You Have Been Freed from Sin to Pursue Holiness

Before you knew Christ, you were a slave to sin; but because of the gospel, you are empowered to pursue righteousness (Romans 6:6–22; 2 Corinthians 5:17). The Bible draws a sharp contrast between your life before Christ and after. Galatians 5:16–26 is a helpful passage that calls you to crucify the desires of the flesh and live by the Spirit. The "flesh" is what the Bible refers to as the lingering effects of sin. Ephesians 4:22–24 says, "Put off your old self ... and be renewed in the spirit of your minds ... and put on the new self." The old self describes a life that dishonors God. Putting on the new self is the process of replacing the old self with thoughts, feelings, and actions that honor God. The renewal of the mind is the divine, progressive, and transformational process of aligning the way you think with Scripture (Romans 12:2; Colossians 3:9–10). Because you have been freed from sin and have had your mind enlightened to the glory of Christ, you are able to understand the will of God and conquer sin in your life.

Love for Jesus Should Be Your Primary Motivation for Holiness

Titus 2:11–14 says Jesus gave His life to redeem and "purify for Himself a people for His own possession who are zealous for good works." God does not want cold-hearted followers. He wants passionate worshipers. When Jesus is your greatest treasure, the pursuit of holiness becomes your joy. Love for Christ should be your primary motivation for pursuing holiness. The pursuit of holiness is a form of worship and will bring joy, but Christ must be the center of any motivation. The right action with the wrong motivation is still wrong. The longer you walk with Christ, the more you will experience that a life motivated by a love for Christ brings the most satisfaction. Remember the gospel and pursue Christlikeness as a response to God's love, but never as a means to earn merit or to be exalted among people.

I hope this letter helped explain how to conform to the image of Christ in a way that is honoring to God and reflective of the gospel. My next letter will explain how to abide in Christ through studying the Bible and applying its truths to your daily life.

PERSONAL REFLECTIONS

In your own words, summarize what you have learned in this letter and describe how it applies to your life.

_____

_____

_____

_____

How does the gospel shape your ability to grow in Christlikeness?

_____

_____

_____

_____

What does it mean to be conformed into the image of Christ?

_____

_____

_____

_____

What is the relationship between God's Spirit and your responsibility?

_____

_____

_____

_____

Why is a Christ-centered motivation necessary for true heart change?

_____

_____

_____

_____

What is your daily plan to grow in Christlikeness this week through the power of God's Spirit?

_____

_____

_____

_____

What other questions do you have?

_____

_____

_____

_____

5

STUDY AND APPLY GOD'S WORD

And now I commend you to God and to the word of His
grace, which is able to build you up and to give you the
inheritance among all those who are sanctified.

ACTS 20:32

I hope this letter finds you doing well and walking in the empowerment of the Spirit that is yours in Christ and that my last letter helped explain how to grow in Christlikeness. In this letter, I want to teach you how to abide in Christ by understanding and applying God's Word in your daily life.

Let the Word of God Abide in You

John 15:7 shows the correlation between abiding in Christ and His Word abiding in you. In Jesus' final prayer before He was arrested, He prayed for God to sanctify believers in the truth of His Word (John 17:17). The Bible is God's divine Word. Second Timothy 3:16 says the Bible is profitable for teaching, reproving, correcting, and training in righteousness. Growing into the likeness of Christ is closely connected to growing in knowledge and obedience to God's Word. This is why reading God's Word is essential to your daily relationship with Christ. Study God's Word with a purpose and with the freedom to go as slow or as fast as you need. Consistency is most important, not speed. Whenever you study God's Word, read it with an open heart and with an expectation that God is going to speak to you through His Holy Spirit.

Understand the Original Meaning of the Text

There are two general principles to follow when reading God's Word: Understand the original meaning and apply it to everyday life. Second Peter 1:20–21 says men under the supernatural inspiration of the Holy Spirit wrote God's Word. God worked through the personalities, cultures, and skills of the authors to inspire every thought, sentence, and word. There was an original purpose to every book, sentence, and word. Only after you grasp the original meaning the author intended to convey, can you apply the truth to your daily life. To understand the original meaning of the passage, you can use the following sequence to study: Context, God, Man, Cross, Response. This is the same sequence you would use to share the gospel with a friend. Questions that follow this sequence could be:

- "What is the context of this passage?"
- "What does this teach me about God?"
- "What does this teach me about man?"
- "How does this passage point to the cross?"
- "How does God expect me to respond to this?"

Asking these five questions will help you understand the biblical text and make application to everyday life. It may also be helpful to study a passage using multiple translations of the Bible, allow other Scriptures to help interpret the original Scripture, and discuss what you are learning with others. I have included additional information for Bible study at the end of these letters.

Apply Biblical Truth to Everyday Life

After you have determined what the author's main point was, you can seek to apply that to your life. Application relates to your mind (how you think), your heart (how you feel), and your actions (how you live). Every passage will relate to all three categories, although not always equally clear. Make application through the lens of the gospel. Ask questions such as, "Because of the gospel, how should this truth affect how I think, feel, and act?" Every time you read Scripture, God expects you to respond in some way. If you are having trouble understanding how it applies, ask God to show you how He wants you to respond and discuss it with a Bible study partner. When you find aspects of your life that are inconsistent with Scripture, simply confess that to God and ask Him to help you align your thoughts, desires, and behavior to be consistent with His truth. Then ask a godly friend to keep you accountable.

Memorization and Meditation Links Bible Study to Prayer

Memorizing Scripture is an important exercise because it will help you grow in knowledge and obedience to God's Word and fight off temptation by claiming God's truth in a moment of weakness. Meditation is the combination of processing biblical truth and seeking to understand it in terms of every day life. Memorization and mediation link Bible study and prayer because it will help you keep God's Word fresh on your mind as you pray.

I hope this letter helped explain how to abide in Christ by understanding and applying God's Word in your daily life. My next letter will teach you about prayer by studying how Jesus taught His disciples to pray.

PERSONAL REFLECTIONS

In your own words, summarize what you have learned in this letter and describe how it applies to your life.

_____

_____

_____

_____

How does the gospel shape your ability to understand and apply God's Word?

_____

_____

_____

_____

What is the process of studying God's Word and making practical application?

_____

_____

_____

_____

How does memorization and meditation link Bible study to prayer?

_____

_____

_____

_____

What is your daily plan to study God's Word?

_____

_____

_____

_____

What other questions do you have?

_____

_____

_____

_____

6

PRAY IN THE NAME OF JESUS

And so, from the day we heard, we have not ceased to pray for
you, asking that you may be filled with the knowledge of His will
in all spiritual wisdom and understanding, so as to walk in a
manner worthy of the Lord, fully pleasing to Him, bearing fruit
in every good work and increasing in the knowledge of God.

COLOSSIANS 1:9–10

I hope this letter finds you doing well and walking in the conviction of God's Word and that my last letter helped explain how to study the Bible and apply biblical truth in your daily life. In this letter, I want to teach you about prayer and how to develop a vibrant prayer life with God.

Prayer Is Communication with God

Communication is essential in any relationship. Prayer is how you communicate with God. The Bible says when you pray to God, He will hear and respond (Psalms 34:17). Learning to discern God's voice from the world's voice can be difficult. When you pray, listen for what God wants to tell you. God will typically speak to you through His Word, the counsel of a mature believer, and feelings of peace or conviction from the Holy Spirit. Regardless of how God speaks, interpret everything in light of what He reveals through His Word. If there is ever any contradiction to what God says in His Word, then you need to reject the counsel or experience and trust completely on God's authoritative Word.

Pray in the Name of Jesus

All religions have their own reasons for praying. Some people pray because of fear of their god. Others think prayer will manipulate a desired outcome from their god. Christians approach the throne of the only true God with confidence through the blood of Jesus Christ (Hebrews 4:16). Christ has accomplished all that was necessary to reconcile you with God, and He now serves as the mediator between God and man (1 Timothy 2:5). This is why when Christians pray, we pray in the name of Jesus.

Follow the Examples in Scripture

In Matthew 6:9–15, Jesus taught His disciples how to pray. We call this the Lord's Prayer or the Model Prayer. The Lord's Prayer has six elements in two categories. The first three are prayers that focus on God: God's praise, God's kingdom, and God's will. The second three are prayers that focus on God's care for you: His provisions for you, His forgiveness for your sins, and His deliverance from evil. Each prayer has multiple applications.

These six prayer emphases can guide you, but Philippians 4:6 also says you should let your requests be known to God. Nothing is too big or too small to present to God; He cares about all things. He wants you to pray in blocks of time set aside for Him in addition to praying unceasingly throughout the day. When you examine the life of Nehemiah, for example, you will see he set aside time to pray and also prayed consistently throughout the day (Nehemiah 1:4–2:5). This is a good example to follow.

Fasting Is an Important Element of Spiritual Growth

Fasting is a Christian's voluntary abstinence from food for a spiritual purpose. The purpose of fasting is to help you draw closer to God by humbling yourself and confessing that your need and desire for God are greater than your need and desire for food. Job stated, "I have not departed from the commandment of His lips; I have treasured the words of His mouth more than my portion of food" (23:12). Jesus expects His disciples to fast (Matthew 6:16), but He puts no time requirements on it. In the Bible, believers typically fast to worship God (Luke 2:37) and seek His guidance (Acts 14:23). You can incorporate fasting into your life this week by choosing to forgo a meal and use that time instead to pray and worship.

Ask God for What You Need

Here is an example of a prayer you could pray before you study God's Word:

Heavenly Father,

Thank You for this time You have given me today to meet with You. I ask that You would be gracious and glorify Yourself during this time. Please quiet my heart and clear my mind to focus, teach me through Your Word, and help me to hear Your voice. Give me wisdom to understand your truth, courage to apply what I learn with joy and boldness, and strength to obey Your commands. Help me abide in Christ today and honor You. In the name of Jesus I pray. Amen.

I hope this letter helped you understand what prayer is and how you can develop a vibrant prayer life with God. My next letter will teach you about worship by studying Jesus' conversation with a Samaritan woman.

PERSONAL REFLECTIONS

In your own words, summarize what you have learned in this letter and describe how it applies to your life.

_____

_____

_____

_____

How does the gospel shape your ability to pray?

_____

_____

_____

_____

How does Bible study and prayer relate to each other?

_____

_____

_____

_____

What does a vibrant prayer life look like for you?

_____
_____
_____
_____

Why are fasting and meditation important elements of spiritual growth?

_____
_____
_____
_____

What is your daily plan to devote yourself to prayer this week?

_____
_____
_____
_____

What other questions do you have?

_____
_____
_____
_____

7

WORSHIP GOD IN SPIRIT AND TRUTH

Ascribe to the Lord, O heavenly beings, ascribe to the Lord
glory and strength. Ascribe to the Lord the glory due His
name; worship the Lord in the splendor of holiness.
PSALM 29:1–2

I hope this letter finds you doing well and walking in the power of the Spirit that is yours in Christ and that my last letter helped explain the role of prayer and fasting in your life. In this letter I want to teach you about worship and how to worship God in spirit and in truth.

True Worship Is Christ-Centered

Worship is outwardly ascribing to God the glory due His name and inwardly valuing Him above everything else. In John 4:7–30, Jesus dialogued with a Samaritan woman about the true meaning and expression of worship. She understood worship in terms of worshipping God in a specific place with a specific ritual. Jesus taught her that worship is not a matter of *where* and *what*, but rather *who* and *how*. Jesus taught her to worship the Father in spirit and in truth.

Worship Begins at Conversion

Worshiping God in spirit simply means that you cherish God in your heart and you are moved with emotion because of His greatness and love. It means your eyes have been opened to the beauty of Christ (2 Corinthians 3:18) and there has been an inward transformation that is reflected through an outward expression. Worshiping God in truth simply means agreeing and reciprocating with how God reveals Himself in His Word.

Think back to your conversion. Your first moment of worship was when you first trusted Christ. In that moment, you embraced the greatness of God and understood that He is worthy to be praised. That is the foundation of worship, and it propels everything else. Your response of trusting Christ was an outward reflection of the love and value you felt for God internally.

True Worship Involves the Heart

In Matthew 15:8–9, Jesus quoted the prophet Isaiah when He referred to the Pharisees of that day. He said they honored Him with their lips, but their hearts were far from Him. He said their worship was in vain. You can do all the right external actions, but if your heart is not near to God, you are not experiencing true worship. There will certainly be times in life when you do not feel moved by God. In that moment, ask God to stir in your heart a longing for Him. The Psalms are filled with these prayers (e.g., Psalms 51).

True Worship Is Demonstrated in Every Area of Life

Worship begins in the mind and heart, and it is reflected in external actions. There are two primary forms of outwardly expressing worship. First, explicitly ascribing to God the glory He deserves (Psalm 29:1-2). As Creator and sovereign Ruler of the universe, God is worthy of all possible praise, honor, and devotion. You do this in singing, writing, and praying. Second, worship is reflecting God's worth in every day life. In Romans 12:1-2, Paul urged believers to present their bodies as living sacrifices as a spiritual act of worship. Worship is not just an external action that has a beginning and an end. It is constantly living a life that reflects the true worth of Christ. When you live this way, you proclaim to the world that Jesus is your greatest treasure, and you are willing to give away all the world can offer, as long as you get Jesus.

True Worship Is Shaped by the Gospel

The glory of God in the gospel is central in all of worship, because the full character of God is revealed in the cross and resurrection. God's love, holiness, justice, and power all culminate at the cross and resurrection. For example, because God is merciful, He provided the cross. Because God is just, He provided the cross. The glory of God in the cross is also central in how we worship every day as a living sacrifice (Romans 12:1). Your example for this is Jesus who lived every day in complete obedience to God. His perfect obedience was on display when He gave all He had and was nailed to the cross. This demonstration of love and obedience is the ultimate example for every believer. Likewise, God's power and authority is demonstrated in the resurrection when Jesus conquered death. It is impossible to fully appreciate and therefore worship God when you fail to remember the cross and resurrection.

I hope this letter helped explain what worship is and how to worship God in spirit and in truth. My next letter will teach you about evangelism and taking the gospel to places and people who have never heard.

PERSONAL REFLECTIONS

In your own words, summarize what you have learned in this letter and describe how it applies to your life.

_____

_____

_____

_____

How does the gospel shape your understanding of and ability to worship God?

_____

_____

_____

_____

What does it practically mean to worship God in spirit?

_____

_____

_____

_____

What does it practically mean to worship God in truth?

_____

_____

_____

_____

What does it practically mean to worship God as a living sacrifice?

_____

_____

_____

_____

What is your daily plan to worship God this week?

_____

_____

_____

_____

What other questions do you have?

_____

_____

_____

_____

8

SHARE THE GOSPEL WITH A LOST WORLD

*All this is from God, who through Christ reconciled us to Himself
and gave us the ministry of reconciliation; that is, in Christ God
was reconciling the world to Himself, not counting their trespasses
against them, and entrusting to us the message of reconciliation.
Therefore, we are ambassadors for Christ, God making His appeal
through us. We implore you on behalf of Christ, be reconciled to God.*
2 CORINTHIANS 5:18–20

I hope this letter finds you doing well and walking in a spirit of genuine worship and that my last letter helped explain how to worship God in every area of life. In this letter, I want to teach you how to share the gospel with your friends, family, and those beyond your shared language and culture.

Evangelism Is Sharing the Good News of Christ

Second Corinthians 5:18–20 says you have a responsibility and privilege to share the good news of Christ with the lost through verbal and nonverbal forms of communication. Evangelism is sharing the gospel of Christ, through the empowerment of the Holy Spirit, with those who have yet to believe, while persuading them to respond by repenting of sin and trusting Christ as Savior and Lord. Gospel proclamation is necessary, for without hearing the gospel first, a person is unable to respond to Christ (Romans 10:13–15). Without a personal decision to trust Christ, a person is and always will remain separated from God (John 3:18; 14:6).

Sharing the Gospel Includes Being a Good Listener

Sharing the gospel requires courage, but it does not have to be complicated. Sharing the gospel is a combination of presenting truth, using illustrations to explain spiritual concepts, and reasoning in a way that is gentle and respectful to each person (1 Peter 3:15). A good evangelist will ask good questions to discover the hearer's preexisting beliefs, explain the gospel in a way that is clear and relevant, listen for obstacles that hinder the hearer from believing, and identify natural "bridges" that help illustrate biblical principles. Being a careful listener will help you know how to best help the other person. A person who is argumentative does not reflect the Spirit of Christ. Reason with grace and patience, while trusting the Holy Spirit to open hearts. Paul demonstrates this routinely in his ministry (Acts 17:2; 17:17; 18:4; 18:19).

Sharing the Gospel Includes Telling Your Personal Testimony

It is helpful to share a personal testimony about how you came to trust Christ as Savior and Lord. This could also be a testimony about how the gospel transforms your life daily. Acts 22:1–21 and Acts 26:1–29 detail the account of Paul's personal testimony of his conversion to Christ. Paul shared what life was like before he trusted Christ, how he came to a decision to trust Christ, and what his life has been like since he trusted Christ as his Savior and Lord. That model is a good one to follow. Personal stories that reflect the gospel illustrate how God wants to be involved with His people.

Missions Is Sharing the Gospel Cross-Culturally

Missions is the act of crossing cultural and linguistic barriers for the purpose of sharing a culturally appropriate gospel presentation with the hope of leading others to saving faith, making disciples, and planting indigenous churches. Missions is necessary because people cannot call on Jesus until they have first heard the gospel. Romans 10:13–15 says a person cannot hear the gospel and have the opportunity to call on His name unless someone is sent to tell them. The church is God's primary agent for sending missionaries to places where the name of Christ has not been named.

God Will Accomplish This Mission through His People

God desires to be glorified among all the peoples of the earth. Revelation 7:9 says one day in heaven there will be a great multitude from every nation, tribe, people, and language worshiping God. Fervent prayer, generous giving, sacrificial going, and utilizing biblical strategies are the only hope of reaching the nations. Man cannot do it alone, but through the empowerment of the Holy Spirit, the gospel will be proclaimed as a testimony to all nations (Matthew 24:14). Still today, there are thousands of people groups that have yet to hear the gospel. Unless someone goes to them, they will never have a chance to trust Christ, because they have never heard the gospel.

I hope this letter helped explain how to share the gospel with your friends, family, and those beyond your shared language and culture. My next letter will teach you about baptism, church membership, the Lord's Supper, and using your gifts to serve the church.

PERSONAL REFLECTIONS

In your own words, summarize what you have learned in this letter and describe how it applies to your life.

_____

_____

_____

_____

How does the gospel shape your ability to share Christ with others?

_____

_____

_____

_____

How would you share your personal conversion testimony with someone?

_____

_____

_____

_____

List five friends and describe your plan for sharing the gospel with
each one this week.

_____

_____

_____

_____

Why is it important for churches to send missionaries?

_____

_____

_____

_____

What is your plan to find out more about mission trip opportunities
through your local church?

_____

_____

_____

_____

What other questions do you have?

_____

_____

_____

_____

9

JOIN AND SERVE THE LOCAL CHURCH

*For just as the body is one and has many members, and all the
members of the body, though many, are one body, so it is with
Christ. For in one Spirit we were all baptized into one body—Jews
or Greeks, slaves or free—and all were made to drink of one Spirit.
For the body does not consist of one member but of many.*
1 CORINTHIANS 12:12–14

I hope this letter finds you doing well and walking in the boldness that
is yours in Christ and that my last letter helped explain the privilege and
responsibility you have as an ambassador of Christ to share the gospel and
advance the kingdom among those who have never heard. In this letter, I
want to teach you about baptism, church membership, the Lord's Supper,
and using your gifts to serve the church.

Baptism Is by Immersion after Conversion

In the Great Commission (Matthew 28:18–20), Jesus commanded that every believer be baptized. The meaning of the word *baptize* is "to immerse." Therefore, biblical baptism is the act of immersing a person who has made a personal decision to trust Christ into water in the name of the Father, Son, and Holy Spirit. This means sprinkling is not a biblical form of baptism. The act of baptism does not provide salvation or build merit with God. Salvation is by grace through faith in Jesus Christ alone (Ephesians 2:8–9). Baptism is a visual and symbolic demonstration of your union with Christ in the likeness of His death and resurrection (Romans 6:4–5). It signifies that your former life has been put to death and that you have been raised to walk in a new life. Baptism serves as a public testimony to the world that you are a follower of Christ, and it is simply following the commands of Christ.

Church Membership Is a Covenant Commitment

First Corinthians 12:12–14 uses the metaphor of a body to teach that every believer belongs to the body of Christ. This global body of believers manifests itself in local churches all around the world. A local church "is an autonomous congregation of baptized believers who are associated by covenant in the faith and fellowship of the gospel."[4] Church membership is a covenant commitment believers make together that expresses their desire to faithfully serve God through that local body. Although the words "church membership" do not appear in Scripture, the meaning is certainly implied (Acts 2:42–47; 1 Corinthians 12:12–14; Ephesians 4:11–16; Hebrews

13:17). Membership in a local church allows you to grow and serve in community with others. Each member provides a specific function to the body. Without each member, the body is disabled and cannot function properly. God has not called you to isolation. When God called you to Himself, He also called you into His family. The local church is the physical manifestation of God's family.

The Purpose of the Lord's Supper Is to Remember Christ until He Comes

Before Jesus was arrested and crucified, He instituted the Lord's Supper so His followers would remember His sacrifice on the cross (Matthew 26:26–29). The Lord's Supper symbolizes the breaking of Christ's body and the shedding of His blood for the penalty of your sin (1 Corinthians 11:23–34). Churches use bread to symbolize Christ's body and either red wine or grape juice to represent His blood. Before participating in the Lord's Supper, you should be baptized, remember Christ's sacrifice and resurrection, examine your own life for unconfessed sin, and recommit to Christian unity in the church. This has been an important tradition in the church for more than two thousand years.

Serve the Church with Spiritual Gifts

God not only called you to belong to a local church, but He also called you to serve the spiritual and physical needs of that local church and surrounding community. There are many ways to serve the church and community. When you received the gospel, you were given various spiritual gifts by the indwelling Holy Spirit for the glory of God and the edification of the church (1 Peter 4:10–11). Edification means helping or instructing as a blessing to someone. You may not know at this time specifically how the Lord has gifted you to serve. That is okay. The important thing is that you get involved doing something. As you serve the many needs of the church, the Lord will show you your gifts, and other believers will affirm it. You have the responsibility and privilege to use the gifts God has given you for His glory, the edification of the church, the benefit of the surrounding community, and your joy.

I hope this letter helped explain baptism, church membership, the Lord's Supper, and using your gifts to serve the church. My next letter will teach you how to faithfully use all you have for the glory of God, the advancement of the gospel, and your joy in Christ.

PERSONAL REFLECTIONS

In your own words, summarize what you have learned in this letter and describe how it applies to your life.

_____

_____

_____

_____

How does the gospel shape your understanding of membership and participation in a local church?

_____

_____

_____

_____

What are the purposes, meanings, and processes of baptism and the Lord's Supper?

_____

_____

_____

_____

How would you practically explain church membership to a friend?

_____

_____

_____

_____

What are some ways you can discover and develop your spiritual gifts by serving in the church?

_____

_____

_____

_____

How do you believe God is calling you to respond to the biblical truths in this letter?

_____

_____

_____

_____

What other questions do you have?

_____

_____

_____

10

STEWARD GOD'S BLESSINGS

The God who made the world and everything in it, being Lord of heaven and earth, does not live in temples made by man, nor is He served by human hands, as though He needed anything, since He himself gives to all mankind life and breath and everything.

ACTS 17:24–25

I hope this letter finds you doing well and serving in a local church and that my last letter helped explain baptism, church membership, the Lord's Supper, and how to serve the church. In this letter, I want to teach you how to steward all that God has given you for His glory, the advancement of His kingdom, and your joy.

God Gives Everything for a Purpose

Everything is from God (John 3:27). Health, money, jobs, family, influence, and relationships are all from God. He intends for you to be a responsible steward of all He has provided and use His gifts for His glory and the advancement of His kingdom (1 Peter 4:10). The primary motivation of stewardship should be to glorify God. Check your motives often. The right action with the wrong heart motive may serve a need but will be displeasing to God. Be careful you do not fall into a man-centered motivation like the Pharisees, who were appealing on the outside and wicked on the inside (Matthew 23:27–28). One day you will stand before the Lord and give an account for your life (2 Corinthians 5:10). This will not be a hearing about your salvation. Christ has already paid the penalty for your sin (Romans 8:1), but God will inquire about the blessings He has provided to you. May you be found faithful on that day.

Steward Your Money for the Glory of God

One of the most difficult areas of life to steward well is money. Jesus said in Matthew 6:21 that you can generally determine what is important to people by how they spend their money. It costs money to do just about everything. It costs money to provide food for someone or to send missionaries to the places where Christ has not been named. It is important to remember the words of Jesus when He said it is more blessed to give than to receive (Acts 20:35). You should carefully steward your money so you can give generously to good causes–starting with the church.

Steward Your Opportunities for the Glory of God

It is not by accident that you are where you are. God has divinely placed you where you are for a specific purpose (Acts 17:26). In His divine wisdom, He not only chose the time period you would be born, but He also determined where you would live and work. Opportunities can be found in both individual moments and seasons. Every day you will have specific opportunities to honor God by sharing the gospel, helping someone in need, etc. These are one-time opportunities that come and go quickly. But you also have opportunities in seasons. This is reflected in your family, job, and residence. These are opportunities that allow you to reflect Christ routinely over an extended period of time.

Steward Your Body for the Glory of God

God will also hold you accountable for the stewardship of your body. First Corinthians 6:18–20 teaches three things about the body: It is a temple of the indwelling Holy Spirit, it was bought with a price, and it should be used to glorify God. Proper eating habits, rest, and exercise, as well as guarding your body against harmful substances and sexually immoral practices, all affect the stewardship of your body.

Steward the Gospel for the Glory of God

In 1 Corinthians 4:1–2, Paul explains his responsibilities as an apostle of Jesus Christ. These responsibilities, though, are also applicable to all believers. Paul said he was a servant of Christ and a steward of the mysteries of God. The mysteries of God start with the gospel message but also extend to the whole Word of God. Paul had four primary objectives throughout his ministry: to proclaim the gospel (Romans 15:20), to teach the whole counsel of God (Acts 20:27), to start churches (Acts 14:23), and to train others to be effective ministers of the gospel by drawing their strengths from the grace that is in Jesus (2 Timothy 2:1–2). Today, these are called evangelism, discipleship, church planting, and leadership development. You should seek to reflect these same objectives in your life and ministry.

I hope this letter helped explain how to steward all that God has given you for His glory, the advancement of His kingdom, and your joy in Christ. My next letter will teach you the difference between worldly truth and Christ-centered truth.

PERSONAL REFLECTIONS

In your own words, summarize what you have learned in this letter and describe how it applies to your life.

_____

_____

_____

_____

How does the gospel shape your ability to steward God's blessings?

_____

_____

_____

_____

How does stewardship glorify God and reflect the worth of Jesus?

_____

_____

_____

_____

What are some practical examples of how God calls you to honor Him with your time and resources?

_____

_____

_____

_____

What are some practical examples of how God calls you to honor Him with your body?

_____

_____

_____

_____

What are some other practical ways God is calling you to be a better steward this week?

_____

_____

_____

_____

What other questions do you have?

_____

_____

_____

_____

PART 2

FOUNDATIONAL CHRISTIAN VALUES

11

CHRIST-CENTERED TRUTH

Jesus answered, 'You say that I am a king. For this purpose I was born and for this purpose I have come into the world— to bear witness to the truth. Everyone who is of the truth listens to my voice.' Pilate said to Him, 'What is truth?'
JOHN 18:37–38

I hope this letter finds you doing well and faithfully stewarding all that God has given you and that my last ten letters helped explain how the gospel shapes foundational practices of the faith. The next ten letters will teach you how the gospel shapes foundational Christian values to be centered in Christ. These values should be incorporated into your life. In this letter, I will teach you about truth, how to recognize truth, and how it should affect how you see the world.

Truth Is Found in God

How do you discern what is truth? In Colossians 2:8–9, Paul warned the church not to be "taken captive by philosophy and empty conceit." This warning applies to you today as well. You can protect yourself against these things by knowing how to recognize truth. Truth is the accurate description of reality as it actually is. Truth transcends space and time, and it is universally binding upon all people everywhere for all time. Truth governs the universe according to the purpose of the Creator. Everything that exists can only be understood fully in light of its Creator, who is God (Genesis 1:1). God is self-sufficient and self-existing. There was no beginning to God. He always was and always will be. God is and forever will be truth. He is the Source of truth, Sustainer of truth, and Revealer of truth. Nonbelievers can understand principles that are true (for example, 1+1=2), but they will never be able to understand the fullness of truth (for example, the creation of life) because they do not know God.

Only Jesus Is Qualified to Reveal Truth

There have been many people who claim to reveal truth, though most of them contradict one another. Truth can only be revealed by the One who knows everything, which is God. In John 14:6, Jesus said, "I am the way, truth, and life. No one comes to the Father except through me." Jesus is the only person who speaks with complete authority about truth, because He is God in the flesh (John 1:14). Colossians 1:15–20 says, everything was created by Jesus, for Jesus, through Jesus, and is held together by Jesus. All answers can be found in Jesus because He is God and all things were created through Him. Also, all things were created for the glory of God. Jesus, as "the radiance of the glory of God and the exact imprint of His nature" (Hebrews 1:3), is the only person qualified to reveal truth because all truth is found in Him.

Jesus Revealed Four Things about Truth

In John 17:1–9, Jesus revealed four things about truth. First, Jesus said there is only one true God. This means all other gods and religions are false. Jesus was establishing that absolute truth is based on who God is and what God has done. Second, He said the gospel is truth. The gospel (the good news of what God has victoriously accomplished for sinners through Jesus Christ) is supreme over all beliefs and philosophies. Third, He said the Bible is truth. The Bible is not just truthful; it is the highest standard of authoritative truth. Fourth, Jesus also said God's people are sanctified in biblical truth. This means you cannot grow in Christlikeness without also growing in knowledge and obedience to God's Word.

Truth Affects How You See the World

Worldview is a concept that explains how a person sees the world. Cultural values, personal experiences, and society can help shape your worldview. As a Christian you should see the world through a biblical worldview. Think of it as seeing the world through the lens of Scripture. This will allow you to determine what is true and what is fiction. Romans 12:2 says, "Do not be conformed to this world, but be transformed by the renewal of your mind, that by testing you may discern what is the will of God, what is good and acceptable and perfect." You allow Scripture to transform your mind by aligning what you think with what Scripture says. When you find your perception of things contradicts what Scripture teaches, then it is important to seek answers as to why that is. It is possible you have misinterpreted what Scripture is truly teaching. Or perhaps you need to realign the way you think about a certain topic with God's authoritative Word.

I hope this letter helped teach you about truth, how to recognize truth, and how it should affect how you see the world. My next letter will teach you about love and the difference between worldly love and Christ-centered love.

PERSONAL REFLECTIONS

In your own words, summarize what you have learned in this letter and describe how it applies to your life.

_____

_____

_____

_____

How does the gospel shape your understanding and pursuit of Christ-centered truth?

_____

_____

_____

_____

What is the difference between the world's perspective and the Christian perspective on truth?

_____

_____

_____

_____

Why are truth and honesty important values for Christians?

_____

_____

_____

_____

What does it practically mean for Christ-centered truth to shape your life?

_____

_____

_____

_____

What is one measurable way you can apply the principles from this letter this week?

_____

_____

_____

_____

What other questions do you have?

_____

_____

_____

_____

12

CHRIST-CENTERED LOVE

For God so loved the world, that He gave His only Son, that
whoever believes in Him should not perish but have eternal life.
JOHN 3:16

I hope this letter finds you doing well and walking in the truth that is yours in Christ and that my last letter helped explain what truth is and how it should shape your worldview. In this letter, I want to teach you about Christian love and how to love God and people.

God Is Love

In Ephesians 2:1–9, the apostle Paul explained that you were once dead in your sins, living according to the passions of your flesh, and were by nature a child of wrath. And then God intervened. Paul writes, "But God, being rich in mercy, because of the great love with which He loved us, even when we were dead in our trespasses, made us alive together with Christ" (vv.4–5). You are called to love and enabled to love because

God first loved you. Love is an orientation of the mind, an emotion of the heart, and an act of the will because of who God is and what God does. It is a result of the gospel, inspired by the gospel, a reflection of the gospel, and for the advancement of the gospel. Your love for God declares that God is infinitely valuable, infinitely glorious, and infinitely worthy of all your praise, admiration, and devotion. Love reflects God because God is love (1 John 4:8). If there is one characteristic that defines who you are, let it be love.

Love God with Your Heart, Soul, Mind, and Strength

Mark 12:28–30 is an important passage that describes what it means to love God. Jesus had two objectives in this dialogue. First, He declared the object of your love should be God and Him alone. Second, Jesus declared you should love God with all your heart, soul, mind, and strength. These four descriptions explain that you are to be fully committed (emotionally, spiritually, intellectually, and physically) to God and Him alone. Jesus is teaching His followers that loving God is more than just actions. Loving God with your entire being is a combination of the mind, heart, and body. You love God with your thoughts by aligning how you think about Him with the way He reveals Himself in Scripture. You love God with your emotions and affections by pursuing Jesus as your greatest delight and abhorring what He deems as evil. You love God with your actions when you obey His commands (1 John 5:1–3). And you love God with your whole life when you offer all you are as a spiritual sacrifice to be used by God for His glory.

Love Your Neighbor as Yourself

Jesus goes on to explain the second commandment in Mark 12:31 when He said, "The second is this: Love your neighbor as yourself." There are three passages that are helpful in understanding this. In Matthew 7:12, Jesus said to treat others the way you want to be treated. In Luke 10:29–37, Jesus explained how to be a good neighbor. First Corinthians 13:4–7 gives many descriptions as to what love is and is not. You are to show the same love to others, even to your enemies (Matthew 5:44), that God shows to you.

Love Believers with a Brotherly Affection

There is a third dimension of love that believers should show to each other. Romans 12:10 says, "Love one another with brotherly affection." The form of love Paul describes here is not found anywhere else in Scripture. It describes the type of warm, heart-felt, sacrificial, loving affection family members should share with each other.[5] You are to love other brothers and sisters in the faith with this same type of affection.

Pursue God When You Don't Feel Love

Scripture is filled with commands that demand your obedience. God does not expect you to obey only when it is convenient; He calls you to obey all the time. There will certainly be times when it is difficult to love. But in that moment, remember the gospel and ask God to help you love.

Don't merely ask that He help you be loving toward a person, but that He would enable your heart to love the way He commands. God desires to fill you with what you do not have for His glory and your joy. God will give you what He commands if you will ask Him for it.

I hope this letter helped teach you about Christian love and how to love God and people. My next letter will teach you the difference between worldly faith and Christ-centered faith.

PERSONAL REFLECTIONS

In your own words, summarize what you have learned in this letter and describe how it applies to your life.

_____

_____

_____

_____

How does the gospel shape your understanding and pursuit of Christ-centered love?

_____

_____

_____

_____

What is the difference between the world's perspective and the Christian perspective on love?

_____

_____

_____

_____

Why is love an important value for Christians?

_____

_____

_____

_____

What does it practically mean for Christ-centered love to shape your life?

_____

_____

_____

_____

What is one measurable way you can apply the principles from this letter this week?

_____

_____

_____

_____

What other questions do you have?

_____

_____

_____

_____

13

CHRIST-CENTERED FAITH

Now faith is the assurance of things hoped for, the conviction
of things not seen ... And without faith it is impossible to
please Him, for whoever would draw near to God must believe
that He exists and that He rewards those who seek Him.
HEBREWS 11:1, 6

I hope this letter finds you doing well and walking in the love that is yours in Christ and that my last letter helped explain how to enjoy the love of God and reflect that love toward others. In this letter, I want to teach you about Christ-centered faith and how it should shape your life.

Faith Defines Worldview

Faith determines everything. What you believe about something shapes and reflects your worldview and answers important questions such as: Where did I come from? What is the purpose of life? What happens after I die? Faith can be defined as belief or trust in a person, system, or object. So what is the difference between worldly faith and Christian faith? The answer is in the object of that faith.

God Is the Center of Christian Faith

To understand Christian faith, it is necessary to understand four things found in two different verses, Hebrews 11:1 and 11:6. Verse 1 says faith is the "assurance of things hoped for." This assurance is a full certainty or confidence in something hoped for. Hope is a combination of something you expect to happen and desire to happen. Verse 1 also says faith is the conviction of things not seen. Conviction is the result of being convinced of something based on proof. If we stop the definition here, it is not much different than the world's definition of faith. Hebrews 11:6 explains what separates worldly faith and Christian faith. Hebrews 11:6 also has two components. Verse 6 says faith must believe God exists, which establishes God as the central object of your faith. It also says faith believes God rewards those who seek Him. In order to truly believe God rewards, one must believe three things about God: First, God is inherently good. He is not an evil god in a pleasant disguise. Everything God has done, is doing, and will do is good. Second, God desires good for His people. It is the foundational belief that in every situation, God has a desire to do good for His children. Third, God is fully able to do what He has promised (Romans 4:21). In summary, Christian faith can be simply defined as the assurance and conviction that God exists, is good, and able to do what He has promised.

Faith Is Essential in Salvation

God chose to redeem you by grace through faith so that you cannot boast in anything else except Jesus (Ephesians 2:8–9). In regard to salvation, faith is believing in Jesus Christ, depending on Him to save you, and trusting He will give you eternal life. You were saved by faith (Ephesians 2:8–9), justified by faith (Galatians 2:16), given righteousness by faith (Philippians 3:9), sealed with the Holy Spirit by faith (Ephesians 1:13), live by faith (Galatians 2:20), and are able to please God because of faith (Hebrews 11:6).

Faith Is Essential in Godly Living

Faith is not just God's plan to save you. It is also God's plan to keep you and draw you closer to Him.

In regard to the life of the believer, faith is believing Jesus is the Author and Perfecter of your faith (Hebrews 12:2), depending on Christ to cover you with grace and forgiveness (1 John 1:9), and trusting God will provide what you need (Matthew 6:11–13). Because of faith in Christ, you have peace with God (Romans 5:1), you stand in God's grace (Romans 5:2), you have access to God (Ephesians 3:12), you are able to draw near to God (Hebrews 10:22), and you hope for the return of Christ (Galatians 5:5).

Faith Shapes Your Character

Faith should affect your character in two ways, and both are because God is faithful (1 Thessalonians 5:24). First, you should have a strong faith in God. When you exhibit faith, you reflect the greatness of God. It means you are fully convinced God is infinitely powerful and able to accomplish all He desires. Second, you should be faithful to keep your promises and do what you say you will do. When you exhibit faithfulness to others, you reflect the character of God.

I hope this letter helped teach you about Christ-centered faith and how it should shape your life. My next letter will teach you the difference between worldly hope and Christ-centered hope.

PERSONAL REFLECTIONS

In your own words, summarize what you have learned in this letter and describe how it applies to your life.

_____

_____

_____

_____

How does the gospel shape your understanding and pursuit of Christ-centered faith?

_____

_____

_____

_____

What is the difference between the world's perspective and the Christian perspective on faith?

_____

_____

_____

_____

Why are faith and faithfulness important values for Christians?

_____

_____

_____

_____

What does it practically mean for Christ-centered faith to shape your life?

_____

_____

_____

_____

What is one measurable way you can apply the principles from this letter this week?

_____

_____

_____

_____

What other questions do you have?

_____

_____

_____

_____

14

CHRIST-CENTERED HOPE

Therefore, since we have been justified by faith, we have peace
with God through our Lord Jesus Christ. Through Him we
have also obtained access by faith into this grace in which
we stand, and we rejoice in hope of the glory of God.
ROMANS 5:1–2)

I hope this letter finds you doing well and walking in the faith that is yours in Christ and that my last letter helped explain what Christian faith is and why it should be an important value in your life. In this letter, I want to teach you the difference between worldly hope and Christ-centered hope.

Christian Hope Is a Confident Expectation and a Joyful Desire

Faith and hope are closely related concepts. In fact, in order to define faith, you have to include an element of hope, "the assurance of things hoped for" (Hebrews 11:1). The difference between these two terms is that hope claims everything faith does, but then takes it one step further. In the last letter I defined faith as the assurance and conviction that God exists, is good, and is able to do what He has promised. Hope shares the same confident expectations as faith, but it also includes a longing desire for God to fulfill His promises. For example, you can have a confident expectation that a sports team will win the game but still hope they don't. Hope is having a confident expectation they will win and a desire for them to win. Hope is the confident expectation of what God has done, is doing, and will do while longing for the day when God will accomplish all that He has promised.

Christ Is the Object and Foundation of Your Hope

In the first chapter of 1 Peter, Peter taught three important things about hope. Verses 3–4 says you have been born again to a living hope by the mercy of God the Father through the resurrection of Jesus from the dead. He is contrasting a living hope to a dead one. You were united to the resurrected Jesus when you were born again by the mercy of God. Jesus is your hope and inheritance. Because Jesus is alive, your hope is alive for eternity. Verse 13 says you are to set your hope fully on the grace that will be revealed at the revelation of Jesus. Hope is the grace of God. It was by God's grace that you were redeemed, it is by God's grace that you are growing, and it will be by God's grace that you will one day be delivered into glory. Verse 21 concludes with the most important point of all. Peter was warning his readers not to place their faith and hope in anything other than God, even the things of God. When the end comes, the greatest joy will be God Himself, not the things He gives you. For example, the Bible describes heaven as paradise. Heaven is only marvelous, though, because of God. If God were not in heaven, it would not be paradise. Eternal life will be eternally satisfying and you will experience the greatest happiness possible because of God, not anything else. Christ makes this possible. He is the object and foundation of hope.

The Glory of God Is the Ultimate Hope for Believers

Scripture calls you to hope for many things: the appearing of Jesus (Titus 2:13); the redemption of your body (Romans 8:23); the hope of righteousness (Galatian 5:5); the deliverance from harm; for His name to be honored, His kingdom to come, and His will be done (Matthew 6:9-13); and for joy and peace so hope can abound (Romans 15:13). But there is one concept that should summarize the hope of the believer—that is the hope of glory. In Romans 8:18-25, Paul said the hardships we suffer in the current age are not comparable to the glory that will be revealed. He goes on to describe how believers, along with creation, inwardly yearn for the day of redemption. You should have a confident expectation and longing for the promises of God to be completed and for all His children to be fully delivered to the glory of God.

The Gospel Provides Hope

In Romans 5:1-2, Paul said, "Therefore, since we have been justified by faith, we have peace with God through our Lord Jesus Christ. Through him we have also obtained access by faith into this grace in which we stand, and we rejoice in hope of the glory of God." There would be no hope without the life, death, and resurrection of Jesus Christ. The gospel not only provides salvation and the hope of glory, but hope for every day. The gospel turns normal, routine days into potential life-changing days. Only the gospel can offer people hope, because only the gospel has the power to transform lives.

I hope this letter helped explain the difference between worldly hope and Christ-centered hope. My next letter will teach you the difference between worldly happiness and Christ-centered joy.

PERSONAL REFLECTIONS

In your own words, summarize what you have learned in this letter and describe how it applies to your life.

_____

_____

_____

_____

How does the gospel shape your understanding and pursuit of Christ-centered hope?

_____

_____

_____

_____

What is the difference between the world's perspective and the Christian perspective on hope?

_____

_____

_____

_____

Why is hope an important value for Christians?

_____

_____

_____

_____

What does it practically mean for Christ-centered hope to shape your life?

_____

_____

_____

_____

What is one measurable way you can apply the principles from this letter this week?

_____

_____

_____

_____

What other questions do you have?

_____

_____

_____

_____

15

CHRIST-CENTERED JOY

Though you have not seen Him, you love Him. Though
you do not now see Him, you believe in Him and rejoice
with joy that is inexpressible and filled with glory.
1 PETER 1:8

I hope this letter finds you doing well and walking in the hope that is yours in Christ and that my last letter helped explain how the gospel defines and shapes hope to be centered in Christ. In this letter, I want to explain what Christ-centered joy is, how it is different than worldly happiness, and how to pursue your joy in Christ.

Joy Is the Result of Delighting in Jesus

Worldly happiness is fleeting. It is based on circumstances that can change instantaneously when the object or source of that happiness is affected. People pursue their happiness in education, jobs, material possessions, and the praise of others. It is true that these things can bring satisfaction and happiness to an extent, but they cannot fully satisfy the soul because the soul was designed to delight in something much greater. As a believer, you know true happiness is directly conjoined to God; this is called joy. Joy is difficult to describe because it is a combination of delight, excitement, gratitude, gladness, confidence, and awe in Christ. However, Christian joy can be defined as a supernatural, unwavering, and spontaneous emotional outflow of the heart because of your delight in who Jesus is and what Jesus has done, is doing, and will do.[6] Unlike worldly happiness, joy is not based on circumstances. It is a result of delighting in Christ, who is unchanging, and a product of the indwelling Holy Spirit (Galatians 5:22–23). Joy is supernatural because it is produced by the Spirit, unwavering because it is anchored in Christ, and spontaneous because it cannot be manipulated or manufactured. It remains stable through the "ups" and "downs" because Jesus is the object and source of delight.

Jesus Is the Object and Source of Joy

The world defines joy as taking great delight in something incredible or satisfying. As you can see, that is not much different than our definition of joy. The only difference is the object and source of that delight. For example, a nonbeliever might delight in a family member's success. There is nothing sinful about this, but it does not grasp the full meaning of what God intended. For Christians, the object and source of joy is Christ. Here are three passages that can help you understand Jesus as the object and source of your joy. First, John 10:10 says Jesus came not only to give life, but life more abundantly. Jesus wants you to experience the most out of life, but He knows this is only possible when you pursue that joy in Him.

Second, in John 2:1–11 Jesus performed His first miracle by turning water into wine. Wine in the Old Testament symbolized God's blessing and joy. Jesus was demonstrating that He is the eternal source of God's blessing and joy. In John 15:11, Jesus said your joy would be full when you delight in Him. Jesus taught that for your joy to be full (to get the most out of life), He has to be the object of your delight.

Pursue Your Joy in Christ

While you cannot command your heart to feel joy, you can pursue things that produce joy. For example, a farmer cannot will a crop to grow, but he can pursue what he can control—plow the field, plant the seed, and depend on God to send the rain. So how do you pursue joy? Here are seven ways Scripture says to pursue your joy in Christ: Abide in Christ through love and faith (1 Peter 1:8); grow in knowledge and obedience to God's Word (John 15:11); flee things that kill your joy and pursue things that increase your joy (2 Timothy 2:22); invest in the spiritual growth of others (2 Corinthians 1:24); rejoice in hope (Romans 12:12); delight yourself in the Lord (Psalm 29); and pray for God to fill you with joy (Romans 15:13). The pursuit of joy requires your active participation, the grace of God, and the power of God's Spirit.

Fight for Your Joy

Joy is the result of delighting in Jesus. Your flesh, the lingering affects of sin, wants to destroy your joy. Your flesh works against you by trying to make you forget the hope you have in Jesus. This is why it is important to remind yourself daily of the promises you have in the gospel. In John 16:22, Jesus told His disciples no one could take their joy from them. Fight for your joy by remembering the gospel and relying on God to sustain you. Press into God by asking Him to fill your heart with joy in Christ.

I hope this letter helped explain what Christ-centered joy is, how it is different than worldly happiness, and how to pursue your joy in Christ. My next letter will teach you how to endure hard situations by setting your eyes on Jesus.

PERSONAL REFLECTIONS

In your own words, summarize what you have learned and describe how it applies to your life.

_____

_____

_____

_____

How does the gospel shape your understanding and pursuit of Christ-centered joy?

_____

_____

_____

_____

What is the difference between the world's perspective and the Christian perspective on joy?

_____

_____

_____

_____

Why is joy an important value for Christians?

_____

_____

_____

_____

What does it practically mean for Christ-centered joy to shape your life?

_____

_____

_____

_____

What is one measurable way you can apply the principles from this letter this week?

_____

_____

_____

_____

What other questions do you have?

_____

_____

_____

_____

16

CHRIST-CENTERED ENDURANCE

Therefore, since we are surrounded by so great a cloud of witnesses,
let us also lay aside every weight, and sin which clings so closely,
and let us run with endurance the race that is set before us,
looking to Jesus, the founder and perfecter of our faith, who for
the joy that was set before Him endured the cross, despising the
shame, and is seated at the right hand of the throne of God.
HEBREWS 12:1–2

I hope this letter finds you doing well and walking in the joy that is yours in Christ and that my last letter helped explain how to pursue your joy in Christ. In this letter, I want to teach you how to endure through difficult situations so you can faithfully persevere to the end (2 Timothy 4:7).

God Uses Hardship for His Glory and Your Good

In John 15:20, Jesus told His disciples they would be persecuted for following Him. After Christ rose from the dead and ascended to heaven, persecution broke out against the church in Jerusalem. Stephen was stoned (Acts 7:58), and the church was scattered. This was to fulfill Jesus' promise that the disciples would be His witnesses starting in Jerusalem and extending to the ends of the earth (Acts 1:8). God allowed hardship in order to fulfill a greater purpose, which was the spreading of the gospel. What man meant for evil, God uses for good (Genesis 50:20). In 2 Timothy 3:12, Paul tells Timothy that anyone who desires to live a godly life in Jesus will be persecuted. As a follower of Christ, you should deal with persecution the same as you deal with other forms of hardship, such as physical illness and natural disasters, by setting your eyes on Jesus, who is the Author and Perfecter of your faith (Hebrews 12:2).

Endure Hardships by Remembering Jesus

In 2 Timothy 2:8–13, Paul taught Timothy how to courageously endure hardship by providing him with five things to remember when he faced hardship. First, he told Timothy to remember Jesus, who was raised from the dead and is the Messiah. Second, he reminded Timothy that while a person can be locked up, the Word of God cannot be bound. It will accomplish what the Lord desires (Isaiah 55:11). Third, Paul endured for those who will receive the gospel. Fourth, he reminded Timothy of the eternal glory that will come at the appearing of Jesus (Romans 8:18). Fifth, Paul reminded him that God cannot deny Himself. At conversion, you were adopted by God the Father, united to God the Son, and indwelt by God the Spirit. You are in Christ, and God will not deny Himself.

God's Grace Is Sufficient for You

In 2 Corinthians 12:7–10, Paul described a personal battle. He said that in order to keep him from becoming conceited, a messenger of Satan was given to harass him. Three times Paul pleaded with God to remove the thorn in his flesh, but God said to him, "My grace is sufficient for you, for my power is made perfect in weakness." The messenger was from Satan, but God permitted him to stay. Satan and God had different motives for this. Satan always seeks to steal, kill, and destroy (John 10:10), while turning God's people away from Him. Satan's purpose was to discourage Paul into giving up. However, God allowed it to remain for two reasons. First, God allowed it to remain to keep Paul humble. God is more concerned with your character than with your comfort (Romans 5:4). Second, God allowed it to remain to exalt Christ. When you face difficult times, your greatest need will not be a quick relief but the grace of God to sustain your through your trial. When you suffer well, you exalt Jesus because you testify to the world that Jesus is your greatest treasure. Keep your eyes set on Jesus and rely on God's strength to persevere.

Boldness Is an Important Element of Endurance

Paul accepted the persecution that came with following Christ, and he used it to fuel his boldness. In Ephesians 6:19, Paul asked the church to pray that he would boldly proclaim the gospel. Throughout Paul's life he was able to do just that (Acts 9:27–28; 28:31; 1 Thessalonians 2:2). For Paul, boldness was an important element of endurance. His goal was not to simply survive but to walk in victory.

I hope this letter helped explain how to endure through difficult situations so you can faithfully persevere to the end. My next letter will teach you about the peace Jesus provides with God, yourself, and with others by explaining how the gospel shapes each of those relationships.

PERSONAL REFLECTIONS

In your own words, summarize what you have learned in this letter and describe how it applies to your life.

_____

_____

_____

_____

How does the gospel shape your understanding and pursuit of Christ-centered endurance?

_____

_____

_____

_____

What is the difference between the world's perspective and the Christian perspective on endurance?

_____

_____

_____

_____

Why is endurance an important value for Christians?

_____

_____

_____

_____

What does it practically mean for Christ-centered endurance to shape your life?

_____

_____

_____

_____

What is one measurable way you can apply the principles from this letter this week?

_____

_____

_____

_____

What other questions do you have?

_____

_____

_____

_____

17

CHRIST–CENTERED PEACE

For in Him all the fullness of God was pleased to dwell, and
through Him to reconcile to Himself all things, whether on
earth or in heaven, making peace by the blood of His cross.
COLOSSIANS 1:19–20

I hope this letter finds you doing well and walking in the perseverance that is yours in Christ and that my last letter helped explain how to endure through difficult times by keeping your eyes on Jesus. In this letter, I want to teach you about the peace Jesus provides with God, yourself, and others.

Jesus Provides Peace through the Cross

Peace is the opposite of conflict, and conflict is everywhere. When Adam and Eve rebelled against God, sin and death entered the world (Romans 5:12). This sinful, rebellious spirit not only caused hostility between man and God, but it has also been passed down from generation to generation and affects every area of your life. It distorts man's view of God, self, and others. Because of sin, guilt and shame remain on every nonbeliever, whether he or she can feel it or not. If you were caught on camera breaking the law, you would be guilty and the government would be just to give you a ticket, even if you unknowingly committed the crime. It is the same with God. When people sin, God is just to condemn them, even if they unknowingly did it. Everyone has sinned, and the weight of guilt and shame hangs over each person. People try to rid themselves of this guilt in different ways. For some, it is religious rituals, while for others it is busyness. Regardless, everyone can feel his or her shame, and all try to remove it. But there is only one way to find peace—Jesus. Jesus came not only to remove the hostility between you and God, but He also came so you could experience God's peace with others.

Jesus Provides Peace with God

Romans 5:1 says, "Since we have been justified by faith, we have peace with God through our Lord Jesus Christ." On the cross, God poured your wrath on Jesus, who willingly died as your substitute. It was God's plan to crush Jesus so that His righteous requirement would be upheld. By placing your sin on Jesus, God removed your guilt and shame. The guilt and shame you rightly deserved for your sin are replaced by the righteousness of Jesus (2 Corinthians 5:21). Your judgment was turned to favor. Jesus removed the wall of hostility between you and God so that you could be reconciled to Him in peace (Ephesians 2:13–16). Because Christ has given you peace vertically with God, you are now able to experience peace with yourself and pursue it horizontally with others.

Jesus Provides Peace with Self

The effects of sin in life are real. When people sin, the shame of failing to honor God affects them. It is one of the ways the Holy Spirit convicts nonbelievers to repent and turn to Christ. But as a believer in Christ, God wants you to experience the peace you rightfully have with Him. When Jesus gave you peace with God, He removed your shame; Jesus wiped you clean. You will still sin (everyone does), but God is faithful to forgive you through the blood of Jesus—if you will repent and ask for forgiveness. The gospel not only made you right with God, but it also keeps you right with God. When you repent, confidently claim the victory Christ has provided to you on the cross (Hebrews 4:16). Your right standing with God is eternal. There is nothing that can separate you from the love of God (Romans 8:38–39). God wants you to experience this peace in your heart, and He has provided it through Jesus.

Jesus Provides Peace with Others

As a believer in Christ, you are a member of God's family and His Spirit lives in you. God desires for all His children to live in peace. You have been shown much grace by God. Withholding grace from others is hypocritical and dishonoring to God. Hebrews 12:14 and Romans 12:18 commands you to strive to live at peace with everyone—as much as you can control. There will be times when you sin against others, as well as times others sin against you. When conflict arises (and it will), remember the gospel and the peace God has given you. Allow these principles to shape your relationship with others. Unfortunately, peace is not always possible. But you should never stop praying for peace or pursuing it. A commitment to peace honors God, reflects the gospel, and allows you to live the life God wants you to have.

I hope this letter helped explain the peace Jesus provides with God, yourself, and others. My next letter will teach you about Christian community and how the gospel shapes your relationship with others.

PERSONAL REFLECTIONS

In your own words, summarize what you have learned in this letter and describe how it applies to your life.

_____

_____

_____

_____

How does the gospel shape your understanding and pursuit of Christ-centered peace?

_____

_____

_____

_____

What is the difference between the world's perspective and the Christian perspective on peace?

_____

_____

_____

_____

Why are peace and reconciliation important values for Christians?

_____

_____

_____

_____

What does it practically mean for Christ-centered peace to shape your life?

_____

_____

_____

_____

What is one measurable way you can apply the principles from this letter this week?

_____

_____

_____

_____

What other questions do you have?

_____

_____

_____

_____

18

CHRIST-CENTERED COMMUNITY

Rather, speaking the truth in love, we are to grow up in every
way into Him who is the head, into Christ, from whom the
whole body, joined and held together by every joint with
which it is equipped, when each part is working properly,
makes the body grow so that it builds itself up in love.
EPHESIANS 4:15–16

I hope this letter finds you doing well and walking in the peace that is yours in Christ and that my last letter helped explain how Jesus provides peace with God, yourself, and others. My next three letters will explain values that are shared in community and how the gospel shapes each one. In this letter, I want to teach you about Christian community and how the gospel shapes your relationship with others.

Community Is Christ-Centered

Christ-centered community is relationships that orbit around Christ. When God called you to faith, He called you into community with Himself and with other believers. Community with God reflects a vertical relationship, while community with other believers reflects a horizontal relationship. Both of these have Christ at the center. Hebrews 4:16 is a reflection of the vertical relationship you have with God, while Ephesians 4:4–16 reflects the horizontal relationships you have inside the body of Christ. A Christ-centered community encourages believers to glorify God by being obedient to Scripture, growing in Christlikeness, and reflecting the gospel faithfully. God did not call you to isolation. He called you to participate in community with others who encourage you in your walk with God.

Fulfilling the Great Commission Requires Community

You cannot be faithful to the commands of Christ in isolation. For example, each dimension of making disciples in Matthew 28:16–20 (the outward expression in going, the symbolic inward transformation in baptism, and the practice of teaching and obeying God's Word) requires community. Take, for example, the command to baptize in the name of the Father, Son, and Holy Spirit. This is first and foremost a command to literally immerse a new believer in water in the name of the Trinity. However, baptism is also the symbolic action of being united to Christ in His death so you can be raised with Him to walk in new life (Romans 6:4–11). The literal baptism does not transform the soul, but it represents a life that has been freed from the enslavement of sin so that you can grow in Christlikeness. Growing in Christlikeness requires the love, support, encouragement, and sometimes correction from other believers. Nobody grows in isolation.

Community Is Shared at Many Levels

Jesus shared community at different levels. In Luke 10:1, He sent out seventy-two laborers, but most commonly He had twelve disciples. Among the twelve He had a smaller circle of three with whom He was most personal. You can reflect these same principles. Community happens at a large level when you gather with other believers for worship, prayer, and the preaching of God's Word. Community also happens in smaller groups of ten to twenty-five people when you meet to share your life with others. Community also exists in accountability groups typically consisting of two to five people. The purpose of these groups is to foster a personal and secure environment where you can be encouraged and sin can be confessed. Accountability groups are most effective when transparency, trust, and grace abound.

Church Discipline Is an Act of Love

In Matthew 18:15–20, Jesus told His disciples how to handle a brother or sister who is unrepentant. This is called "church discipline." Church discipline is the process of helping those who have fallen into sin repent and repair their relationships with the Lord and with those they have wronged. It includes confronting those in sin, praying for those who fall, encouraging the unrepentant to repent, making restitution for any harm caused, and restoring those who have repented. Every action of church discipline is to be done in love, respect, and patience. The ultimate goal of church discipline is for unrepentant persons to truly repent of their sins before the Lord and to provide healing and reconciliation to relationships that have been damaged. Although church discipline is difficult, it is the most loving thing you can do for those who stray. It cannot exist without community.

I hope this letter helped explain Christian community and how the gospel shapes your relationship with others. My next letter will teach you about the importance of unity in the church and how it reflects a life changed by the gospel.

PERSONAL REFLECTIONS

In your own words, summarize what you have learned and describe how it applies to your life.

_____

_____

_____

_____

How does the gospel shape your understanding and pursuit of Christ-centered community?

_____

_____

_____

_____

What is the difference between the world's perspective and the Christian perspective on community?

_____

_____

_____

_____

Why is community an important value for Christians?

_____

_____

_____

_____

What does it practically mean for Christ-centered community to shape your life?

_____

_____

_____

_____

What is one measurable way you can apply the principles from this letter this week?

_____

_____

_____

_____

What other questions do you have?

_____

_____

_____

_____

19

CHRIST-CENTERED UNITY

So if there is any encouragement in Christ, any comfort
from love, any participation in the Spirit, any affection and
sympathy, complete my joy by being of the same mind, having
the same love, being in full accord and of one mind.
PHILIPPIANS 2:1–2

I hope this letter finds you doing well and cultivating Christ-centered community in your life and that my last letter helped explain why community is necessary for spiritual growth. In this letter, I want to teach you the importance of unity in the church and how it reflects a life changed by the gospel.

Unity Is Impossible without Humility

Unity is an important Christian value because it reflects the unity that is shown in the Trinity as each member works harmoniously together in your redemption. For there to be unity in the church, each member must possess a spirit of humility. In Philippians 2:1–11, Paul charged the church to follow the example of Christ, who modeled humility for His followers. Humility has a vertical and horizontal dimension. Humility is vertical in that it is obedience to God and horizontal in that it seeks to serve the interests of others. An appearance of humility can be faked. This is called "false humility," but true humility genuinely reflects the character of Christ. There is only authentic unity in the church when there is genuine humility among believers. The key to humility is contentment in Christ (Philippians 3:7–11).

Unity Pursues Forgiveness

Conflict disrupts unity. When conflict happens, reconciliation and forgiveness must be pursued. Although forgiveness can be difficult, it is necessary. Forgiveness is the act of sending something away, pardoning an action, or forgetting a debt. Withholding forgiveness from another is a terrible thing–both for you and the other person. Ephesians 4:32 says to "forgive one another, as God in Christ forgave you." This verse clearly illustrates the vertical and horizontal relationship in forgiveness. At conversion, God's forgiveness can be thought of as judicial forgiveness (Ephesians 1:7). Judicial forgiveness would be like a judge pardoning a criminal for his or her crime. Daily forgiveness for the believer can be thought of as parental forgiveness (1 John 1:9). Parental forgiveness would be like a father forgiving his child for a personal offense. When you find you have wronged another, you should repent, take responsibility, and seek to reconcile the relationship. Forgiveness reflects God. Forgive, because God first forgave you.

Unity Only Honors God When Christ Is the Center

Church unity is a collective act of worship toward God by His people. It is a declaration that the church is united in one spirit and one mind for one purpose—the glory of God. Unfortunately, though, this does not always happen. You have to be careful to keep Christ as the center of your unity. God is not honored when unity is regarded as more important than He is. Unity is only celebrated when the church is united around Christ. If the church is united around something that dishonors God, then unity is not worth celebrating. It should be condemned. For example, if a church teaches something that contradicts God's Word, then the church should not be unified around that teaching. There should be division. Unity around things that contradict God's Word doesn't honor God; it dishonors Him. Do all you can to pursue unity (Ephesians 4:1–6), but realize that sometimes God calls His people to graciously rebuke those in sin (2 Timothy 4:2–4). Be careful you do not allow cultural values to cause you to dishonor God by promoting unity over God. Unity is only honoring to God when Christ, not man, is at the center.

There Is Unity in Diversity

Unity does not mean uniformity. One of the metaphors that Scripture uses to describe the church is the body of Christ. In 1 Corinthians 12:12–30, Paul described the church as a diverse group of people, each with unique spiritual gifts. Each and every spiritual gift is for the glory of God and the edification of the body. Unity occurs when diverse people harmoniously worship God with one mind and one spirit. When diverse people join together to worship and serve God as a unified body, they serve as an example to the lost of the love of God and the transforming power of the gospel. This type of unity is reflected in Revelation 7:9 when all ethnicities from all time gather around the throne of God to worship Him.

I hope this letter helped explain the importance of unity in the church and how it reflects a life changed by the gospel. My next letter will teach you about partnerships and how the gospel should compel you to partner with others for God's glory.

PERSONAL REFLECTIONS

In your own words, summarize what you have learned and describe how it applies to your life.

_____

_____

_____

_____

How does the gospel shape your understanding and pursuit of Christ-centered unity?

_____

_____

_____

What is the difference between the world's perspective and the Christian perspective on unity?

_____

_____

_____

_____

Why are unity, humility, and forgiveness important values for Christians?

_____

_____

_____

_____

What does it practically mean for Christ-centered unity to shape your life?

_____

_____

_____

_____

What is one measurable way you can apply the principles from this letter this week?

_____

_____

_____

_____

What other questions do you have?

_____

_____

_____

_____

20

CHRIST-CENTERED PARTNERSHIP

I thank my God in all my remembrance of you, always in every
prayer of mine for you all making my prayer with joy, because
of your partnership in the gospel from the first day until now.
PHILIPPIANS 1:3–5

I hope this letter finds you doing well and walking in Christ-centered unity with others and that my last letter helped explain how to pursue unity by making Christ central. In this letter, I want to teach you about partnerships and how the gospel should compel you to partner with others for God's glory.

Partnerships Reflect the Spirit of Christ

Unity in the local church and partnerships among the global church are both important and reflective of the Spirit of Christ. The global church includes all churches around the world. Churches today, although holding to many different doctrinal positions, can still find ways to work together. Because of these differing doctrinal positions, churches are not able to do everything together. However, churches certainly can find ways to partner that do not compromise the biblical convictions of the other. Partnerships among churches are a practical solution to many obstacles the world faces today and are a reflection of the transforming power of the gospel.

Partnership Has Many Forms

In Paul's ministry, there are four different types of partnerships. First, we see him collecting money from Gentile churches for impoverished Jewish believers in Jerusalem (Romans 15:25–27; 1 Corinthians 16:1–4; 2 Corinthians 8–9). Second, we see the development of prayer partners in many of his letters (Philippians 1:19; Colossians 4:3; 1 Thessalonians 5:25). Third, the church in Philippi sent Epaphroditus to care for Paul (Philippians 2:25–30). Fourth, the church in Philippi supported Paul financially for the advancement of the gospel (Philippians 4:15). In fact, part of Paul's purpose in writing the letter of Romans was to ask for their partnership in the advancement of the gospel to Spain (Romans 15:24). These are not the only forms of partnership, but they are partnerships every church should have.

CHRIST-CENTERED PARTNERSHIP

Biblical Convictions Define Partnerships

Church partnerships exist at different levels and are based on doctrinal convictions. There are many doctrines in the Christian faith. There are some things Scripture is very clear on and the church will not compromise. For example, justification by grace through faith in Jesus Christ is clearly taught in Scripture, but it is also the fundamental disagreement between the Protestant church and the Catholic Church. Because of this doctrinal disagreement about how a person is saved, Protestants and Catholics cannot partner together for evangelism and church planting. However, they can partner to meet the social needs of the community and protect the rights of the unborn against abortion. Sometimes, two churches may agree on how a person is saved but disagree how a church should be planted. These two churches can partner together for evangelism but not church planting. In some situations, though, churches may agree with each other on evangelism and church planting. These two churches can work together for any project, including sending missionaries.

The Gospel Is the Purpose of Partnerships

The purpose of partnerships is to advance the gospel for the glory of God. Even when the service project is meeting social needs, the purpose of that activity is to spread the gospel. Whether it is providing food, building roads, meeting educational needs, etc., the goal is to share the gospel. There are still many people and ethnic groups who have never heard the name of Christ. Every church is called to be faithful to the Great Commission. It is difficult for a small church to send missionaries cross-culturally. Partnerships allow churches to pull resources together so that missionaries can be sent and churches can be planted. Planting a church in a foreign context is a difficult task. It requires a long-term commitment from the missionary and the sending church. Partnering churches can provide missionaries with the necessary prayer, financial, and volunteer team support so their efforts will be effective. Churches can always do more together than on their own. Partnerships make things easier by sharing the responsibility and burden with each other so more people can be reached with the gospel.

I hope this letter helped explain ministry partnerships and how the gospel should compel you to partner with others for God's glory. My next letter will teach you about the Bible and explain how God divinely inspired every word.

PERSONAL REFLECTIONS

In your own words, summarize what you have learned and describe how it applies to your life.

_____

_____

_____

_____

How does the gospel shape your understanding and pursuit of Christ-centered partnership?

_____

_____

_____

_____

What is the difference between the world's perspective and the Christian perspective on partnership?

_____

_____

_____

_____

Why are partnership, cooperation, and conviction important values for Christians?

_____

_____

_____

_____

What does it practically mean for Christ-centered partnership to shape your life?

_____

_____

_____

_____

What is one measurable way you can apply the principles from this letter this week?

_____

_____

_____

_____

What other questions do you have?

_____

_____

_____

_____

PART 3

FOUNDATIONAL CHRISTIAN BELIEFS

21

THE BIBLE

All Scripture is breathed out by God and profitable for teaching,
for reproof, for correction, and for training in righteousness, that
the man of God may be complete, equipped for every good work.
2 TIMOTHY 3:16–17

I hope this letter finds you doing well and partnering with others for the sake of the gospel and that my last ten letters helped you understand how the gospel shapes foundational Christian values. The next ten letters will explain how Christ is central in foundational Christian beliefs. Having a firm conviction about these beliefs will help you protect yourself and the church from false teachings. In this letter, I want to teach you about the Bible as the divinely inspired Word of God and how it points to Jesus (John 5:39).

Scripture Is Divinely Inspired by God

In 2 Timothy 3, the apostle Paul exhorted Timothy to continue trusting the Scriptures. In verse 16, Paul told Timothy all of Scripture is "breathed out" by God. Peter wrote in 2 Peter 1:20–21 that the authors of Scripture spoke from God as they were carried along by the Holy Spirit. These passages are teaching that authors under the supernatural influence of the Holy Spirit wrote every book of the Bible, thus ensuring that the Bible is God's true Word. The Holy Spirit supernaturally worked through the personalities, cultures, and skills of every author while divinely inspiring every word in the original manuscripts.

Divine Authorship Was the Standard for the Canon

The Bible was written over a period of sixteen hundred years by about forty different authors. In the fourth century, church leaders gathered to determine what books and letters were to be included in the "Canon." The word *canon* means measuring rod. The church leaders' goal was to measure each letter and book to see if it met the standard of divine authorship. This was the standard as to whether a book or letter would be included in the Canon. These leaders carefully sought the Lord's will through prayer and discussion. The writings that met the standard of divine authorship were gathered together and that is what we today consider the Bible. Although early church leaders were instrumental in this process, God was sovereign over what books and letters were ultimately included in the Bible. The Bible includes sixty-six books. There are thirty-nine books from the Old Testament and twenty-seven from the New Testament. Every book is the divine Word of God.

The Bible Is God's Authoritative Word

Hebrews 4:12 says the Bible is living and active, and able to penetrate and discern the thoughts and intentions of the heart. Paul in 2 Timothy 3:16–17 goes on to say all of Scripture is "profitable for teaching, for reproof, for correction, and for training in righteousness" so that every believer can grow to maturity in Christ. In regard to these truths, there are five characteristics about Scripture I want to teach you. First, it is completely true and free from error. This is called *inerrancy* and means every word is true and meaningful. Second, the Bible is sufficient for life and godliness. Christian books can be helpful, but the Bible is sufficient to teach you everything you need to know about following Christ. Third, although there are parts of Scripture that can be confusing, everything can be understood clearly through the help of the Holy Spirit (John 16:13). God's Word is meant to bring clarity, not chaos. Fourth, the Bible is complete. There will never be anything that needs to be revised, removed, or added to Scripture (Revelation 22:18). This means there will never be a new revelation. Fifth, the Bible, as God's divine Word, is authoritative and the ultimate standard for all conduct, doctrine, and opinion.

The Glory of God in the Gospel of Jesus Christ Is the Central Theme of Scripture

The Bible is God's revelation of Himself to mankind and includes His expectations for us. All of Scripture testifies to the glory of God and the worthiness of His name to be praised. God's plan from Genesis to Revelation was to redeem for Himself a people through the blood of His

Son so they can worship and enjoy Him for eternity. The central theme of all of Scripture is the glory of God in the gospel of Jesus Christ. The Old Testament describes and points toward the promised Messiah who would redeem God's people from their sins (Deuteronomy 18:15,18). The New Testament describes the life, death, and resurrection of Christ, and it provides instruction to believers as they live out the gospel in everyday life. This means Jesus, who is the radiance of the glory of God, can be found in every passage of Scripture.

I hope this letter helped explain the Bible as the divinely inspired Word of God and how it all points to Jesus. My next letter will teach you about God and how He reveals Himself as the Father, Son, and Holy Spirit.

PERSONAL REFLECTIONS

In your own words, summarize what you have learned and describe how it applies to your life.

_____

_____

_____

_____

How does the gospel shape your understanding of the Bible?

_____

_____

_____

_____

How did God divinely inspire every word of the Bible?

_____

_____

_____

_____

How does both the Old Testament and New Testament point to Jesus?

_____

_____

_____

_____

What does it practically mean to submit to the authority of the Bible?

_____

_____

_____

_____

What is one measurable way you can apply the principles from this letter this week?

_____

_____

_____

_____

What other questions do you have?

_____

_____

_____

_____

22

THE TRIUNE GOD

'You are my witnesses,' declares the Lord, 'and my servant whom I have chosen, that you may know and believe me and understand that I am He. Before me no god was formed, nor shall there be any after me. I, I am the Lord, and besides me there is no Savior.'
ISAIAH 43:10–11

I hope this letter finds you doing well and walking under the authority of God's Word and that my last letter helped explain how the Bible was written under the inspiration of the Holy Spirit and how it points to Christ. In this letter, I want to teach you how God reveals Himself as the Father, Son, and Holy Spirit.

God Is Triune

Isaiah 43 clearly teaches there is one and only one living and true God. He is an intelligent, spiritual, and personal being (John 4:24). As the Creator and supreme Ruler of the universe (Acts 17:24–26), God is infinite in holiness and all other perfections (1 Peter 1:15–16). God is all-powerful and all knowing (Isaiah 46:9–10). His perfect knowledge extends to all things past, present, and future. He is eternally worthy of all possible praise, honor, and glory. To Him you owe the highest love, reverence, and obedience. The eternal triune God reveals Himself in Scripture as the Father, Son, and Holy Spirit, each with distinct personal attributes but without division of nature, essence, or unity (Matthew 28:19).[7] This is called the Trinity or "three in one." The Trinity works harmoniously together while executing different functions in the work of creation and redemption. Each person in the Trinity is fully and completely God.

The Father Is God

The first person in the Trinity is God the Father (Matthew 23:9). God the Father sovereignly reigns with providential care over His universe, His creatures, and the whole flow of human history according to the purpose of His grace and glory. He is infinite, eternal, and personal. He is perfect in holiness, wisdom, power, and love. He is sovereign over all His creation. He is faithful to His every promise, expresses His love toward mankind, has given His Son, Jesus Christ, for the redemption of man, hears and responds to the prayers of His people, foreknows all that will come to pass, blesses His church with every spiritual blessing, and will save from sin all who come to Him through Jesus Christ (John 3:16; John 6:40). He made all things for the praise of His glory and intends for man to live in fellowship with Him. He is fatherly in His attitude toward all men.

The Son Is God

The second person in the Trinity is God the Son, who is Jesus Christ. Jesus Christ, God's only begotten Son, was conceived by the Holy Spirit, born of the virgin Mary, lived a perfect and sinless life, performed many supernatural miracles, and taught with divine authority. He is fully God and fully man (John 1:14). He was always with God and is God. He is the image of the invisible God (Colossians 1:15). He should be worshipped, loved, served, and obeyed by all as Lord. He died as your substitute on the cross as the atoning sacrifice for your sin (Romans 3:25). His death on the cross was God's plan for upholding divine judgment and demonstrating His glorious grace. His death appeased God's wrath, removed your guilt, and reconciled you to God (Romans 5:10). The atonement of His death was sufficient for the sins of the whole world. However, only through person-ally receiving Christ can a person be saved from sin. After being dead for three days, Christ rose from the dead, appeared to over five hundred wit-nesses, provided many convincing proofs for His resurrection, ascended to heaven, and sat at the right hand of God where He intercedes for His people. He will one day return and establish His eternal kingdom on earth.

The Holy Spirit Is God

The third person in the Trinity is God the Holy Spirit. The Holy Spirit is equal with the Father and the Son as God. The Holy Spirit has always been at work in the world by sharing in the work of creation and inspiring the writing of the Bible (2 Peter 1:21). The Holy Spirit convicts the world of sin, righteousness, and judgment (John 16:8). The Holy Spirit regenerates, sanctifies, helps, teaches, empowers, and dwells within God's people (John 3:5; John 14:16; 2 Timothy 1:14). He provides spiritual gifts, produces spiritual fruit, and seals you as a guarantee until the final day of redemption (Galatians 5:22–23; Ephesians 1:13–14).

I hope this letter helped explain how God reveals Himself as the Father, Son, and Holy Spirit. My next letter will teach you about the origin of man, the nature of sin, and how sin has affected every part of your life.

PERSONAL REFLECTIONS

In your own words, summarize what you have learned and describe how it applies to your life.

_____

_____

_____

_____

How does the gospel shape your understanding of the Trinity?

_____

_____

_____

_____

What does it mean that God is three in one?

_____

_____

_____

_____

What does it mean that the Father, Son, and Sprit are equal in value but have different roles?

_____

_____

_____

_____

How do your beliefs about the Trinity shape how you see the world?

_____

_____

_____

_____

What is one measurable way you can apply the principles from this letter this week?

_____

_____

_____

_____

What other questions do you have?

_____

_____

_____

_____

23

THE DEPRAVITY OF MAN

And you were dead in the trespasses and sins in which you once
walked, following the course of this world, following the prince
of the power of the air, the spirit that is now at work in the sons
of disobedience—among whom we all once lived in the passions
of our flesh, carrying out the desires of the body and the mind,
and were by nature children of wrath, like the rest of mankind.
EPHESIANS 2:1-3

I hope this letter finds you doing well and striving to walk in holiness and that my last letter helped explain who God is and how each member of the Trinity works together to accomplish the will of God. In this letter, I want to teach you about the origin of man, how sin separates a person from God, and how sin affects every part of your life.

Man Is Created in the Image of God

The first chapter of Genesis records how the world began. Verses 26–28 record the creation of man: "So God created man in His own image, in the image of God He created him; male and female He created them." To be created in the image of God means many things. Included is the ability to understand rational and moral things. But, it also means that you, as an image bearer of God, reflect the glory of God. When Adam and Eve sinned, which is called the *fall*, their ability to reflect the image of God was defaced. The original design God had for mankind was marred by the stain of sin. Every human being is made in the image of God and is thus deserving of dignity and respect, but only those who have been redeemed by the gospel are able to be restored into the image of God through Christ (Romans 8:29).

Sin Has Separated Man from God

Through the temptation of Satan, man voluntarily transgressed the command of God and sinned. This rebellion resulted in eternal separation from God. Isaiah 59:2 says, "Your iniquities have made a separation between you and your God, and your sins have hidden His face from you so that He does not hear." Sin is the act of dishonoring God by failing to live up to God's standard. Sin is any thought, action, or feeling that contradicts God's Word, character, or will. You sin when you desire, value, or honor anything or anyone more than you desire, value, or honor God. Sin is anything that offends God. The fall resulted in all mankind inheriting a sinful nature from Adam. Every person has inherited this sinful nature and has voluntarily sinned against God. Thus, every person is deserving of eternal punishment. As soon as a person is capable of moral action, he or she becomes a transgressor and is under condemnation.

Man Is Totally Depraved

Every part of unregenerate man has been affected by sin, which renders every person totally depraved. The effects of sin extend to a person's mind, will, and actions. This corrupt nature is an outflow of a person's depraved heart, which is full of deceit and evil (Jeremiah 17:9). First Corinthians 2:14 says the things of God are folly to those who are unregenerate. Second Corinthians 4:3–4 says an unregenerate man is blinded and unable to see the light of the gospel of Christ. However, depravity does not mean man is as sinful as he could be. Before you were regenerate you were able to do loving things and discern the difference of good and evil because you were created in the image of God. But every area of your life was totally affected by and enslaved to sin (Romans 6:6).

Man Is Enslaved to Sin

Because of the effects of sin, unregenerate man lives in bondage to self-reliance, self-justification, self-worth, and self-gratification. Every thought, action, and emotion is sinful because it lacks faith, and whatever does not proceed from faith is sin (Romans 14:23). He is unable to effectively seek, submit, fear, love, desire, or serve God because of sin (Romans 3:11). He is by nature a child of wrath, a hater of God, dead in his trespasses, and a slave to sin (Ephesians 2:3). Unless God graciously intervenes, a person will never turn from his or her rebellion against God. An unregenerate man is unable to reform himself, reconcile his relationship with God, or understand the good news of the gospel. Therefore, God must overcome a person's resistance and inability to understand spiritual things by regenerating the heart and effectually calling that person by His grace. This redeeming work is achieved by the predetermined plan of God, the atonement of Christ, the regenerative work of the Holy Spirit, and the proclamation of the gospel.

I hope this letter helped explain the origin of man, how sin separates a person from God, and how sin affects every part of your life. My next letter will teach you about the gospel of Jesus Christ and the importance of sharing it with those who are lost.

PERSONAL REFLECTIONS

In your own words, summarize what you have learned and describe how it applies to your life.

_____

_____

_____

_____

How does the gospel shape your understanding of man's depravity?

_____

_____

_____

_____

What does it mean that you are created in the image of God?

_____

_____

_____

_____

What is sin and how has it affected every person?

_____

_____

_____

_____

How do your beliefs about sin and man shape how you see the world?

_____

_____

_____

_____

What is one measurable way you can apply the principles from this letter this week?

_____

_____

_____

_____

What other questions do you have?

_____

_____

_____

_____

24

THE GOSPEL OF JESUS CHRIST

For there is no other name under heaven given
among men by which we must be saved.
ACTS 4:12

I hope this letter finds you doing well and walking in humility and that my last letter helped explain why sin alienates a person from God and affects every area of life. In this letter, I want to teach you how God redeems sinners by grace through the life, death, and resurrection of Jesus Christ.

The Gospel of Jesus Christ

The gospel is the story of God's plan to reconcile sinners to Himself in Christ and make all things new. The good news of the gospel is what God has victoriously accomplished for sinners through the birth, life, death, resurrection, ascension, and future return of Jesus Christ. In regard to sharing the gospel, a complete gospel presentation can be simply communicated by addressing four key elements: God, Man, Cross, and Response. Here is an example of that:

God. There is one true God; He is infinitely holy, while perfectly loving and just. As Creator and supreme Ruler, God determines the purpose of His creation and sets the standard by which man must live, which is complete devotion to Him. But man rebelled. Sin is the act of dishonoring God. Because of the fall, every part of man has been affected by sin.

Man. Man is a wicked, selfish sinner who continually dishonors God and is thus deserving of God's wrath (Romans 3:23). The result of sin is death, and the due punishment is eternal destruction (Romans 5:18; 6:23). But God, who is rich in mercy (Ephesians 2:4), sent His Son, Jesus, to be the penal, substitutionary atonement of sin so man can be forgiven and reconciled to God (2 Corinthians 5:18, 21).

Cross. Jesus, conceived by the Holy Spirit and born of the virgin Mary, lived a sinless life, was fully God and fully man, performed many miracles, willingly died on the cross, and was raised from the grave on the third day (1 Corinthians 15:4). Jesus' death on the cross was a substitutionary and propitiatory sacrifice that satisfied the demands of God's perfect justice and removed His holy wrath by paying the debt of sin in full (Colossians 2:13–14; 1 Peter 2:24; 1 John 2:2). The cross was necessary, for without the shedding of blood, there cannot be forgiveness for sin (Hebrews 9:22).

Response. This salvation is offered freely to everyone who will repent and trust Christ (Acts 20:21). One day Jesus will return and judge the world in righteousness. Those who have never trusted Christ will be punished with everlasting destruction in hell, but those who have believed in Christ will enter into eternal joy with God. The cross of Jesus is the grace of God (Ephesians 2:8).

Receive the Gospel through Repentance and Faith

People cannot be saved by their good works or sincere efforts, but only by the grace of God through repenting of their sins and making a personal decision to trust Christ in faith (Mark 1:15). Repentance is recognizing you are a sinner, confessing your need for God's forgiveness, and consciously turning from sin toward God. Faith is believing in Jesus Christ, depending on Him to save you, and trusting He will give you eternal life. A commitment of your entire will to Christ as Savior and Lord is necessary.

Salvation Is Found Exclusively in the Gospel

In John 14:6, Jesus said, "I am the way, and the truth, and the life. No one comes to the Father except through me." The gospel of Jesus Christ is the only message of salvation. This means no other gospel, system of faith, religious practice, or name other than Jesus can provide salvation to sinners (Acts 4:12). Every person must make an explicit and personal decision to trust Jesus Christ in order to receive God's salvation. In Romans 10:13–15, Paul said people must first hear the gospel in order to repent of their sins and believe in Christ. Therefore, personal evangelism and cross-cultural missions should be an important priority in your life and in the life of every believer and church.

Those Who Belong to Christ Will Persevere to the End

You are secure in your salvation for eternity because it is God who gives eternal life through Jesus Christ. Salvation is established and maintained by the grace and power of God, not by your self-effort. In John 10:27–29, Jesus said, "My sheep hear my voice, and I know them, and they follow me. I give them eternal life, and they will never perish, and no one will snatch them out of my hand." At conversion, you were united to Christ and are secure in Him for eternity. If you are truly a believer, you will persevere to the end. You may fall into sin by neglect and temptation, but there will be conviction that leads you to repentance.

I hope this letter helped explain how God redeems sinners by grace through the life, death, and resurrection of Jesus Christ. My next letter will teach you how each person of the Trinity works harmoniously together for your salvation.

PERSONAL REFLECTIONS

In your own words, summarize what you have learned and describe how it applies to your life.

_____

_____

_____

_____

How did this letter help you better understand the gospel?

_____

_____

_____

_____

What does it mean to repent and trust Christ?

_____

_____

_____

_____

What does it mean that salvation is only found in Jesus?

_____

_____

_____

_____

Why will those who trust Jesus never lose their salvation?

_____

_____

_____

_____

What is one measurable way you can apply the principles from this letter this week?

_____

_____

_____

_____

What other questions do you have?

_____

_____

_____

_____

25

GOD'S WORK IN SALVATION

There is therefore now no condemnation
for those who are in Christ Jesus.
ROMANS 8:1

I hope this letter finds you doing well and walking in the grace that is yours in Christ and that my last letter helped explain how God redeems sinners by grace through faith in Jesus Christ. In this letter, I want to teach you how each person of the Trinity works harmoniously together for your salvation.

God the Father Chose You in Him before the Foundation of the World

In Ephesians 1:4, Paul told the believers in Ephesus that before the world began, God chose them to be holy and blameless in Christ. This was true for them then and true for you today. This is called the *doctrine of election*. Election is the predetermined and sovereign decision and action of God to choose those who will be saved. This election is unconditional, meaning that God's choice was not based on any conditions you had to achieve in order to be chosen. It is not based on any good that you did or any future action or decision you would do, but only on God's good pleasure and will (Romans 9:11; 2 Timothy 1:9). This does not devalue or nullify the reality and importance of your free will.[8] You had to make a personal and voluntary decision to repent of your sins and trust Christ, but somehow God was mysteriously sovereign over that process (John 6:37–44).

This is one of the most difficult doctrines of the Christian faith because not everyone will be saved. However, God cannot be blamed or deemed unfair. True fairness would mean God allowing all who have rebelled against Him to receive their due consequences, which is eternity in hell.[9] Choosing even one person to save is an eternally significant act of mercy. God is holy and just and is right to punish sinners for their sins. Your response to this doctrine should be thankfulness, humility, and reverence (2 Thessalonians 2:13). In love, God intervened to do what was impossible for any person to do.

The Atonement of Christ Sufficiently Paid the Penalty of Sin

In the Old Testament, the priests made sacrifices to God for the sins of the people (Exodus 29:36). However, Jesus was the promised Messiah who, once for all, atoned for sin (Hebrews 9:28; 1 Peter 3:18). The atonement of Christ is the substitutionary sacrifice Christ made on the cross for God's chosen people. In essence, He purchased your salvation through His suffering (1 Peter 2:24). Christ's redemptive work was sufficient for the sins of all, though efficacious only for God's elect. In some sense Christ died for all, but not all the same way. The atonement of Christ did not just provide common grace to all; rather, it guaranteed the redemption of God's chosen people. Common grace is grace that all people benefit from, which is not the same as saving grace. There is no work or good deed left for you to do in order to be redeemed; the atonement of Christ sufficiently accomplished all that was necessary. The atonement was necessary because God is just. He rules and judges the earth in accordance with His holy character. Because He is just, it is impossible for Him to ignore iniquity and not punish sin. Christ's atonement was a propitiation for the sins of the elect, thus satisfying God's perfect justice and holy wrath (Romans 3:23–25; 1 John 2:2).

The Holy Spirit Regenerates the Hearts of God's People

Regeneration is the divine work of God in which He causes an unregenerate person to be spiritually "born again" by regenerating the heart (John 3:3–8). It is a mysterious and divine work of God that enables the person to recognize and respond to spiritual things (John 6:44). This transformation occurs through the Spirit of God, by the will of God, and as a result of hearing the Word of God. Regeneration will result in saving faith and a heart that loves God (Ezekiel 36:26–27). Although regeneration is an instantaneous event, it will produce spiritual fruit for the remainder of your life.[10] Those whom God regenerates will find God's grace irresistible. This does not contradict or violate a person's voluntary decision to receive or reject Christ.[11] Although a person may show resistance for a time, God's Spirit will eventually overcome that person's resistance and he or she will voluntarily turn to Christ through faith and repentance. Therefore, anyone who wants to be saved can be saved (Romans 10:13). The desire to be saved is proof of the Spirit's regenerative work in a person's heart. This is how God worked in your life to elect, purchase, and call you to salvation. Your salvation is to the praise of God's glory (Ephesians 1:5–6).

I hope this letter helped explain how each person of the Trinity works harmoniously together for your salvation. My next letter will teach you about the many spiritual blessings that are yours in Christ through God's salvation.

PERSONAL REFLECTIONS

In your own words, summarize what you have learned and describe how it applies to your life.

_____

_____

_____

_____

How does the gospel shape your understanding of God's work in your salvation?

_____

_____

_____

_____

What does it mean that God chose you before the foundation of the world?

_____

_____

_____

_____

What does it mean that the atonement of Christ sufficiently paid for the sins of God's elect?

_____

_____

_____

_____

What does it mean that the Holy Spirit regenerates the heart of God's people?

_____

_____

_____

_____

What is one measurable way you can apply the principles from this letter this week?

_____

_____

_____

_____

What other questions do you have?

_____

_____

_____

_____

26

GOD'S SPIRITUAL BLESSINGS IN SALVATION

Blessed be the God and Father of our Lord Jesus Christ, who has blessed us in Christ with every spiritual blessing in the heavenly places, even as He chose us in Him before the foundation of the world, that we should be holy and blameless before Him. In love He predestined us for adoption as sons through Jesus Christ, according to the purpose of His will, to the praise of His glorious grace, with which He has blessed us in the Beloved.

EPHESIANS 1:3–6

I hope this letter finds you doing well and walking in the mercy that is yours in Christ and that my last letter helped explain how each member of the Trinity worked together for your salvation. In this letter, I want to teach you about the many spiritual blessings that are yours in Christ through God's salvation.

God Has United You to Christ

At your conversion, God united you to Christ (Romans 6:5) and you are now eternally secure in Him (2 Corinthians 5:17). This is called *union with Christ*. Union with Christ is God's divine plan to save and preserve His people by placing them in Christ. All the blessings God's people receive are due to God's predetermined plan to unite them to His Son for eternity. This union is expressed through your faith in Christ, and it is the basis for your justification, adoption, sanctification, perseverance, and glorification (Galatians 2:20). Union with Christ is the foundation that all other blessings are built on.

God Has Justified You by Faith

Galatians 2:16 says "a person is not justified by works of the law but through faith in Jesus Christ." This is called *justification*. Justification is the instantaneous and divine work of God to count a person forgiven of sin, pardoned from His impending wrath, and declared righteous in His eyes.[12] From the moment you trusted Christ, you had a positive, peaceful, and right-standing relationship with God in Christ (Romans 5:1). Christ bore your sins on the cross; in turn, God's wrath was turned to favor (2 Corinthians 5:21; 1 Peter 2:24). On the cross, God regarded Jesus as your sin, meaning your sin was imputed to Jesus. Now, God regards Christ's righteousness as your own, meaning the righteousness of Christ was imputed to you. When God sees you now, He no longer sees the stain of sin, but rather the righteousness of Christ. A person cannot be justified by works of the law or good deeds, but only by faith in Christ (Galatians

2:16). This does not mean your faith builds merit with God. Your faith is a result of the regenerative work God has already done in your heart. God's justification is a one-time legal and relational declaration that proclaims you righteous for eternity (Colossians 2:14; Romans 8:1). It is legal in that God's wrath is appeased and relational in that you have been united to Christ and adopted as God's child.

God Has Adopted You into His Family

"Adoption" is the divine work of God in which He accepts into His family those who were once wicked sinners, thus becoming their heavenly Father while considering them beloved sons and daughters (John 1:12; Romans 8:15–17; Ephesians 1:5). As God's child you can enjoy the many blessings associated with being a member of God's family, such as having a personal relationship with God, freedom from the fear of enslavement to sin, the joy of living as an heir to God's blessings, and the eager expectation to one day be with God for eternity.

God Is Sanctifying You through His Spirit and Word

Titus 2:14 says that Jesus not only died to redeem His people but also to purify them. *Sanctification* is the process, beginning at conversion, by which the believer is enabled to progressively become more like Christ through the presence and power of the indwelling Holy Spirit (Romans 8:13, 29).

God Will Give You a Glorified Body

When the bodies of believers are raised from the dead, at the time Christ returns, they will be perfect and glorified bodies (Philippians 3:21). These glorified and imperishable bodies are a reflection of the glory of God and will not be affected by sin, sickness, suffering, disease, or aging. They will perfectly reflect the radiance and glory of God found in the image of Christ for eternity (1 Corinthians 15:49). This is called *glorification*. Glorification will be the eternal physical state of every believer (Romans 8:30).

I hope this letter helped explain the many spiritual blessings that are yours in Christ through God's salvation. My next letter will teach you about the church, her purpose, church leadership, and your responsibility to seek out opportunities to serve.

PERSONAL REFLECTIONS

In your own words, summarize what you have learned and describe how it applies to your life.

_____

_____

_____

_____

How does the gospel shape your understanding of God's spiritual blessings in salvation?

_____

_____

_____

_____

What does it mean that God has united you to Christ?

_____

_____

_____

_____

What does it mean that you are justified before God?

_____

_____

_____

_____

What does it mean that you have been adopted into God's family?

_____

_____

_____

_____

What is one measurable way you can apply the principles from this letter this week?

_____

_____

_____

_____

What other questions do you have?

_____

_____

_____

_____

27

THE CHURCH

So then you are no longer strangers and aliens, but you are fellow
citizens with the saints and members of the household of God,
built on the foundation of the apostles and prophets, Christ Jesus
himself being the cornerstone, in whom the whole structure,
being joined together, grows into a holy temple in the Lord.
EPHESIANS 2:19–21

I hope this letter finds you doing well and walking in a spirit of thanksgiving and that my last letter helped explain the many spiritual blessing that are yours in Christ. In this letter, I want to teach you about the church, her purpose, church leadership, and your responsibility to serve.

Jesus Is the Cornerstone and Head of the Church

In Matthew 16:13–20, Jesus asked His disciples the two following questions: "Who do the people say I am?" and "Who do you say that I am?" Peter responded by saying, "You are the Christ, the Son of the living God." Jesus affirmed Peter's profession and said, "I tell you, you are Peter, and on this rock I will build my church." There is some debate about what Jesus' exact meaning was in this statement, but Peter explained how he understood it in Acts 4:11–12 when he said, "This Jesus is the stone that was rejected by you, the builders, which has become the cornerstone." The cornerstone is the most important stone in the foundation of a building. It keeps everything aligned and stable. Paul reiterates this meaning in Ephesians 2:19–22 when he said the church is built on the foundation of the apostles and prophets, with Christ being the Cornerstone. Paul later wrote that Jesus is the Head of the church (Ephesians 5:23). The church, which was purchased with Jesus' blood, belongs to Jesus. He is the Cornerstone and the Head.

A New Testament Church Operates under the Lordship of Jesus

A New Testament church of the Lord Jesus Christ is an autonomous local congregation of baptized believers who recognize themselves as a church. They are associated by covenant in the faith and the fellowship of the gospel.[13] They observe the two ordinances of Christ (believer's baptism and the Lord's Supper), and they are to submit themselves to the authority of the Scriptures. Each church should strive to reach people with the gospel, make Christ-centered disciples, and plant Christ-centered churches, while serving the physical and spiritual needs of their communities. Each church operates under the Lordship of Jesus Christ through the leadership of the elder body (Hebrews 13:17).

Every Church Needs Biblically Qualified Leaders

There are three groups of people in the church: members, deacons, and elders. Members are baptized believers who understand they are called to a higher degree of responsibility and service in the church and gladly enter into covenant with one another to do that. They voluntarily and joyfully agree to publicly live out a commitment to God, the gospel, their families, and the church. They also understand they have a privilege and responsibility to use the spiritual and material gifts the Lord has given them to serve the church. Deacons are the lead servants of the church. They serve the spiritual and physical needs of the church and its ministries. Elders are the highest human authority of the church. They are biblically qualified men with the responsibility of leading, teaching, governing, mentoring, protecting, and caring for the church. They are tasked with overseeing all church activities and equipping the members to share in the responsibilities of the ministry (Ephesians 4:12). While both men and woman are gifted for service in the church, the office of elder (also known as pastor) is limited to men, as qualified by Scripture (1 Timothy 3:1–7).[14]

Christ Gave the Church Leaders to Equip You to Serve

The local church is God's chosen instrument to fulfill His mission on earth. As a believer, one of the ways you join God in His mission is committing to and serving in a local church. There are many functions of the church, including worship, teaching, prayer, community, discipleship, evangelism, service, giving, ministry, and cross-cultural missions

(Acts 2:42–47). For a church to be faithful to these things, it requires the faithfulness of every member. Ephesians 4:11–16 says Jesus gave church leaders so they could equip the saints (church members) for ministry. This means if a church is to reach its full potential, it requires every member to contribute and serve. As this happens, not only will the church be built up to maturity in Christ but many needs will also be met. God never intended for the elder and deacon body to do everything. It is your responsibility to seek out opportunities to serve Christ and allow elders and deacons to help you.

I hope this letter helped teach you about the church, her purpose, church leadership, and your responsibility to serve. My next letter will teach you about God's design for the family and the role of each family member.

PERSONAL REFLECTIONS

In your own words, summarize what you have learned in this letter and describe how it applies to your life.

_____

_____

_____

_____

How does the gospel shape your understanding of the church?

_____

_____

_____

_____

What does it mean that Jesus is the Cornerstone and Head of the church?

_____

_____

_____

_____

What is a church and why should you belong to one?

_____

_____

_____

_____

What are the qualifications and responsibilities for each of the three groups of people in the church?

_____

_____

_____

_____

What is one measurable way you can apply the principles from this letter this week?

_____

_____

_____

_____

What other questions do you have?

_____

_____

_____

_____

28

FAMILY

Hear, O Israel: The Lord our God, the Lord is one. You shall love the Lord your God with all your heart and with all your soul and with all your might. And these words that I command you today shall be on your heart. You shall teach them diligently to your children, and shall talk of them when you sit in your house, and when you walk by the way, and when you lie down, and when you rise.

DEUTERONOMY 6:4–7

I hope this letter finds you doing well and growing in your love for the local church and that my last letter helped explain what a church is and your responsibility to commit and serve. In this letter, I want to teach you about biblical gender roles, family, marriage, and parenting.

Men and Woman Are Created Equal
but Serve Different Functions

The Bible says God created Adam and Eve in His image and for His glory (Genesis 1:27; 2:4–25; Isaiah 43:7). Men and women are created equal in value and worth, yet different in role and function (1 Peter 3:7).[15] Distinctions in manhood and womanhood are ordained by God and are manifested in the differing functions men and women have in the home and church. These distinctions are established based on the creation order and are God's original design for mankind (1 Corinthians 11:8). Adam's headship over his wife was established before the fall and is reaffirmed after the fall in both the Old and New Testaments (Genesis 3:16; 1 Corinthians 11:3). Because of sin, God's original design for manhood and womanhood was distorted. However, because of Christ's sacrifice on the cross, God's original design can be redeemed (2 Corinthians 5:17). Denial of these biblical truths will result in destructive circumstances for your marriage, family, church, and society. By faithfully honoring Scripture, you honor God.

Family Takes Priority over Your Job and Ministry

God has ordained the family as the foundational institution of human society (Genesis 1:28).[16] It is composed of persons related to one another by marriage, blood, or adoption. An earthly family is a picture of your heavenly family—with God as your Father (Romans 8:15). You honor God when you live as a faithful family member by serving the physical and spiritual needs of your family. First Timothy 3:4–5 requires an elder of a church to first be able to faithfully lead his own family before he can be considered for church leadership. Typically, when believers get too busy, they neglect their spiritual walks and families. Be careful you do not become so busy you neglect your family. If you do, you will voluntarily disqualify yourself to serve for a season.

Marriage Is a Picture of Your Union with Christ

Marriage is the uniting of one man and one woman in covenant commitment for a lifetime (Ephesians 5:22–33; Hebrews 13:4). It is God's unique gift to reflect the union between Christ and His church for eternity (Ephesians 5:32). The husband and wife are of equal worth before God, since both are created in God's image, but they serve different roles (Genesis 1:27). A husband is to love his wife as Christ loved the church (Ephesians 5:25). He has a God-given responsibility to provide for, protect, and lead his family. A wife is to graciously submit herself to the servant leadership of her husband, just like the church willingly submits to the headship of Christ. The wife has the God-given responsibility to respect her husband and to serve as his helper in managing the household and nurturing their children. Marriage also provides the framework for intimate companionship and the means for procreation of the human race. Sex is a meaningful and important part of the marriage relationship. It is a gift from God but should be expressed only in a marriage relationship where there is commitment and trust (Galatians 5:19–21).

Children Are a Blessing from God

Children, from the moments of conception, are a blessing from the Lord (Psalms 127:3; 139:13).[17] This is why abortion is a sin, and the unborn should be protected. If you or someone you know has committed abortion, there is grace at the throne of God if you will repent and ask for forgiveness. Parents are to model for their children a Christlike example in marriage and daily living (Deuteronomy 6:7). They are to teach their children spiritual and moral values through loving discipline and godly instruction (Ephesians 6:4). Children are to honor and obey their parents (Ephesians 6:1; Colossians 3:20).

I hope this letter helped explain biblical gender roles, family, marriage, and parenting. My next letter will teach you about death, heaven, hell, and Satan.

PERSONAL REFLECTIONS

In your own words, summarize what you have learned in this letter and describe how it applies to your life.

_____

_____

_____

_____

How does the gospel shape your understanding of family?

_____

_____

_____

_____

How are men and women equal in value and worth, yet different in role and function?

_____

_____

_____

_____

How is your earthly family a picture of your heavenly family?

_____

_____

_____

_____

How is marriage a picture of your union with Christ?

_____

_____

_____

_____

What is one measurable way you can apply the principles from this letter this week?

_____

_____

_____

_____

What other questions do you have?

_____

_____

_____

_____

29

AFTER LIFE

For if, because of one man's trespass, death reigned
through that one man, much more will those who receive
the abundance of grace and the free gift of righteousness
reign in life through the one man Jesus Christ.
ROMANS 5:17

I hope this letter finds you doing well and walking in the goodness of God's design for you and that my last letter helped explain God's design and purpose for gender roles, family, marriage, and parenting. In this letter, I want to teach what the Bible says about death, heaven, hell, and Satan.

To Live Is Christ, and to Die Is Gain

In Philippians 1:19–26, the apostle Paul wrote about two conflicting desires he had. Paul was in prison, and the possibility of his imminent death was not far away. Yet he was not concerned about death. In fact, his chief concern was that Christ would be honored, whether it was in his death or life. Paul wrote in verse 21–24, "For to me to live is Christ, and to die is gain. If I am to live in the flesh, that means fruitful labor for me. Yet which I shall choose I cannot tell. I am hard pressed between the two. My desire is to depart and be with Christ, for that is far better. But to remain in the flesh is more necessary on your account." Paul did not fear death, and neither should you. Paul knew that the moment of his departure from this life would send him face-to-face with Jesus in heaven.

Death Entered the World through Sin

Death is a result of the fall, where sin entered the world and death followed (Romans 5:12). Death should not be feared by believers, for their spirits will immediately go to be with the Lord (2 Corinthians 5:8). It is appropriate to grieve the passing of a loved one who was also a believer, but you should not grieve as one without hope (1 Thessalonians 4:13). When believers die, their spirits will leave their physical bodies and enter into the presence of the Lord, which is in heaven. At that time, their spirits will be made perfect.[18] Their bodies will remain in the ground until they are resurrected as perfect glorified bodies and reunited with their spirits for the final judgment. However, the passing of nonbelievers should bring great sorrow. At the point of death, the spirit of a nonbeliever will be sent to a place of constant torment until it is reunited with the body for the final judgment. A person will not have a second chance to receive Christ after death (Hebrews 9:27).

Heaven Is the Dwelling Place of God

Scripture speaks of heaven as a place where God is continually worshiped, Christ intercedes for His sheep, the citizenship of the redeemed is found, and the treasures of God's people are stored (Isaiah 66:1; Philippians 3:20). Heaven is also the gathering place of angels. Angels are spiritual beings created by God to worship Him and accomplish His will. When believers die on earth, their spirits immediately ascend to heaven and meet God face-to-face (Luke 23:43). They will remain there in God's presence until the appointed time when God will make all things new.[19]

Hell Is a Place of Eternal Torment

Hell is a literal and eternal place. Scripture describes hell as a place of unquenchable fire, eternal torment, outer darkness, everlasting punishment, and a place of weeping and gnashing of teeth (Matthew 3:12; 2 Peter 2:4). After the final judgment, Satan, his followers, and all who have not received Christ will be consigned to hell for eternal conscious punishment (Revelation 20:10; 21:8).

Resist Satan and Oppose His Schemes

As a believer in Christ, you do not need to fear Satan, but you do need to be aware of his schemes. As the prince of the power of the air, his spirit is at work in nonbelievers (Ephesians 2:2). Satan is a created being who seeks to oppose God, yet is inferior to God in every way. Satan seeks to accuse, deceive, blind, enslave, and destroy God's people (Zechariah 3:1; John 8:44). You should resist Satan, refuse his lies, and oppose his schemes by being filled with the Holy Spirit, praying, and claiming the promises of God's Word (James 4:7). Demons are evil spirits who are followers of Satan. One day Satan and his followers will be thrown into the lake of eternal fire where they will be tormented for eternity (Revelation 20:10).

I hope this letter helped explain what the Bible says about death, heaven, hell, and Satan. My next letter will teach you about the return of Christ, the final judgment, and the consummation of all things.

PERSONAL REFLECTIONS

In your own words, summarize what you have learned in this letter and describe how it applies to your life.

_____

_____

_____

_____

How does the gospel shape your understanding of life after death?

_____

_____

_____

_____

What will happen to your spirit at death?

_____

_____

_____

_____

What is the difference between heaven and hell?

_____

_____

_____

_____

Who is Satan and how can you oppose his schemes?

_____

_____

_____

_____

What is one measurable way you can apply the principles from this letter this week?

_____

_____

_____

_____

What other questions do you have?

_____

_____

_____

_____

30

LAST THINGS

He who testifies to these things says, 'Surely I am
coming soon.' Amen. Come, Lord Jesus!
REVELATION 22:20

I hope this letter finds you doing well and walking in the assurance that is yours in Christ and that my last letter helped explain the hope you have in Jesus now and for eternity. In this letter, I want to teach about the return of Christ, the final judgment, and the consummation of all things.

Proclaim the Gospel to All Nations

One day Jesus will return to establish His eternal kingdom on earth. No one knows the exact time these things will happen, but you should expect it and be ready. Jesus expected His disciples to know about end-time events but not give more attention to them than necessary. Each time Jesus was asked about the end times, He answered the question but then turned the attention to the advancement of the gospel. For example, in Matthew 24:3–14, Jesus described the end times but then said, "And this gospel of the kingdom will be proclaimed throughout the whole world as a testimony to all nations, and then the end will come" (v. 14). In Acts 1:6–8, the disciples asked Him about the end times, and He responded by telling them they will be His witnesses in Jerusalem, Judea, Samaria, and to the end of the earth. In the same way, you should be familiar with teachings about the end times, but let your primary focus be on advancing the gospel.

Christ Will Return to Earth

There are many questions about the end times. Scripture is clear about some things, while being vague on others. One of the things Scripture clearly teaches is that Christ will return in glorious fashion! There are five characteristics concerning the return of Christ you need to know. First, it is a future return; it has not yet happened (Hebrews 9:28). Second, it will be visible for all to see (Acts 1:11). Third, He will return in His physical body (1 John 3:2). Fourth, It will be Jesus Himself who returns (Revelation 22:12). Fifth, it will be glorious (1 Thessalonians 4:16). There is much debate, however, on when Jesus will return, especially in regards to the "millennium" mentioned in Revelation chapter 20. It is good to be aware of this debate but not consumed by it. The important thing is that Christ will return and there will be a final judgment—so be ready.

Be Ready for the Final Judgment

The final judgment is the day God has determined to judge the world in righteousness through Christ. At this time, the bodies of both believers and nonbelievers, of all time, will be resurrected and united to their spirits. Every person will stand before Christ to be judged. The final judgment will do two things. First, Jesus will separate the believers from nonbelievers (Matthew 25:33). Those who have believed in Christ will enter into eternal happiness with God, but those who never trusted Christ will be punished with everlasting destruction and shut out from the presence and glory of the Lord forever (2 Thessalonians 1:9). Second, He will reward believers to various degrees based on their earthly stewardship and punish nonbelievers to various degrees for their sins (Luke 20:47; 1 Corinthians 3:14–15).[20]

Your Joy Will be Eternal and Ever-Increasing

At this time, death will be destroyed (1 Corinthians 15:26) and God will set everything new. This is called the *consummation*. There will be a new heaven and a new earth. Revelation 21:3–4 says God will dwell with man on earth and He will be their God. He will also "wipe away every tear from their eyes, and death shall be no more, neither shall there be mourning, nor crying, nor pain anymore, for the former things have passed away." You will live face-to-face with God without the hindrance of sin, death, pain, or any evil thing; thus, allowing you to enjoy Him forever. Ephesians 2:4–7 says God saved you and seated you in the heavenly places with Christ "so that in the coming ages He might show the immeasurable riches of his grace in kindness towards us in Christ Jesus." The riches of

God cannot be measured because they are infinite. It will take eternity to comprehend the greatness and kindness of God. Each day of eternity will be more intriguing, more interesting, and more satisfying than the day before. There will be no boredom, only ever-increasing fulfillment. You will delight yourself in God with eternal happiness and ever-increasing joy. Your satisfaction in God will never plateau, for God is infinitely great and worthy to be praised!

I hope this letter helped explain the return of Christ, the final judgment, and the consummation of all things. My final letter will teach you about your role in fulfilling the Great Commission.

PERSONAL REFLECTIONS

In your own words, summarize what you have learned in this letter and describe how it applies to your life.

_____

_____

_____

_____

How does the gospel shape your understanding of last things?

_____

_____

_____

_____

Why is it important to advance the gospel to all nations?

_____

_____

_____

_____

_____

How would you explain the return of Christ and the final judgment to a friend?

_____

_____

_____

_____

What does it mean to have ever-increasing joy in heaven?

_____

_____

_____

_____

What is one measurable way you can apply the principles from this letter this week?

_____

_____

_____

_____

What other questions do you have?

_____

_____

_____

_____

PART 4

GO AND MAKE DISCIPLES

31

GO AND MAKE DISCIPLES

*And Jesus came and said to them, 'All authority in heaven
and on earth has been given to me. Go therefore and make
disciples of all nations, baptizing them in the name of
the Father and of the Son and of the Holy Spirit, teaching
them to observe all that I have commanded you.'*
MATTHEW 28:18–20

I hope this letter finds you doing well and longing for the future return of
Jesus and that my thirty letters explaining how the gospel shapes foundational practices, values, and beliefs have helped you understand how
to make Christ central in your life. In this final letter, I want to teach you
about the privilege and responsibility God has entrusted to you—to go and
make disciples of all nations.

Follow the Example of Jesus

The Great Commission (Matthew 28:18–20) is a call for every believer to make disciples. God is calling you to help new believers trust the gospel daily, abide in Christ, and make disciples themselves. In other words, He is calling you to teach new believers the foundational practices, values, and beliefs of the Christian faith so they too can love and treasure Christ. There is much we can learn from Jesus about making disciples. Here are four basic practices from the life of Christ that will help you make disciples.

1. Jesus Prayed for His Disciples

In John 17:1–26, Jesus prayed for His disciples and all those who would come to faith. That includes you. Jesus prayed you would be kept in God, your joy would be full, and you would be sanctified in God's Word. We see this practice reflected in the life of the apostle Paul as well. In each letter, Paul let his disciples know he was praying for them. Life is a spiritual battle. Nothing of eternal value will happen unless God graciously intervenes. Prayer asks God to do what only He can do–bring victory.

2. Jesus Served His Disciples

A few hours before Jesus was arrested, He knelt down and washed the feet of His disciples to show His love for them. He was demonstrating what it means to serve with a servant's heart. In John 15:15–16, Jesus told

His disciples He was setting an example for them to follow. Jesus came to serve, not be served.

3. Jesus Set a Good Example for His Disciples

In Luke 10:1–12, Jesus sent His disciples out in pairs to proclaim the kingdom of God. He told the disciples to allow "persons of peace" to serve their physical needs, so that in return they could serve the spiritual needs of their hosts. The disciples knew how to do these things because they had first witnessed Jesus doing them. Jesus did not ask His disciples to do anything He had not first modeled for them Himself. In the same way, model for others before you expect them to do it.

4. Jesus was Relational with His Disciples

When Jesus called His disciples to follow Him, He was not inviting them to study His life. He was inviting them to do life with Him. The apostle Paul understood discipleship requires sharing your life with someone. In 1 Thessalonians 2:1–12, we see words like *gentle, nurturing, affectionate, exhortation, encouragement,* and *charge* that show how Paul cared for people. There is a spirit of respect, genuine concern, transparency, and love. Discipleship is not a curriculum to be taught or a task to be completed. It is a life-on-life friendship that enables both people to be mutually encouraged to pursue their joy in Christ.

The most important part of the discipleship process is opening your life to others so they can see how the gospel affects how you think, feel, and act. They need to see what it looks like to treasure Christ in everyday life. They need someone who can encourage them to set their eyes on Jesus and love Him with all their hearts, souls, minds, and strength. You do not have to know everything about the Bible to disciple someone; you never will. You simply have to be one step ahead in your journey with Christ so you can show the next person how to follow. By the grace of God and through the empowerment of the Holy Spirit, you should eagerly seek to glorify God by making disciples as you go through life.

I hope this letter helped explain the privilege and responsibility God has entrusted to you—to go and make disciples of all nations. I want to end these letters in the same way Paul closed in 1 Thessalonians 5:23–24 when he said, "Now may the God of peace Himself sanctify you completely, and may your whole spirit and soul and body be kept blameless at the coming of our Lord Jesus Christ. He who calls you is faithful; He will surely do it." Amen.

PERSONAL REFLECTIONS

In your own words, summarize what you have learned in this letter and describe how it applies to your life.

_____

_____

_____

_____

What is your plan to continue meeting with your discipleship partner for ongoing encouragement?

_____

_____

_____

_____

What does it mean to be a Christ-centered disciple?

_____

_____

_____

How does making disciples reflect a Christ-centered life?

_____

_____

_____

_____

Who are three people you want to invest in and teach to follow Christ, and when can you discuss this with each one?

_____

_____

_____

_____

What other questions do you have?

_____

_____

_____

_____

CONCLUSION:
A LIFELONG CALL TO
DIE AND LIVE

So, we've come to the end. Does completing this study make you a disciple of Jesus? The simple answer is "maybe." To be a disciple of Christ is to be a follower of Christ, meaning you are seeking to learn and reflect the beliefs, values, and practices of Christ, stirring your heart to joyful obedience. Discipleship is the process of learning to turn all things in life to point to Christ by allowing the gospel to shape how you think, feel, and act to be centered in Christ. It is a lifelong call to die to self and live fully for Christ. It is not a matter of behavior modification but of heart change.

Everything in life is pointed at something. As a believer in Christ, you have been set free from the enslavement to sin, but that does not mean your life has been automatically centered in Christ. Your thoughts, affections, and actions all point to something—either a self-centered motive or Christ. Christ-centered discipleship is the process of learning to analyze every thought, feeling, and action in light of Christ and trusting God's Spirit to change your life to be like His as you depend on His daily grace with the same tenacity, humility, and dependency you trusted Him with at conversion. You participate in this process by bringing your heart, soul, mind, and strength, through the power of God's Spirit, into alignment with God's will by allowing the gospel to shape every area of your life to be centered in Christ. The Christ-centered life is motivated by love for Christ, obedient to the commands of Christ, modeled after the life of Christ, and empowered by the Spirit of Christ. It is the life that makes Jesus the Source of strength, Object of affection, and ultimate Prize, both during the journey and at the end. That is what it means to be a disciple.

I again mention this in closing because there is a temptation to associate discipleship with head knowledge. Just because you know the right answers about Jesus does not mean you follow Jesus. A disciple follows Jesus. Perfection is not the goal; it's impossible to get there. Growing Christlikeness is the goal, no matter how slow or messy that becomes. If that's true, then discipleship is not about completing a study but being set on a path. To say one has been "discipled" should not imply that person has reached the end, like a terminal doctoral degree, but rather, one has been given the tools needed to grow in Christlikeness. And my sincere hope is that these letters have helped you do just that—to love Jesus more and establish a plan to help others do the same.

Living the Christ-centered life—a life that undeniably reflects Jesus—is difficult, and it is easy to become discouraged. But I don't think you would have made it to the conclusion if you didn't already have a deep conviction that it is God's will for you to be conformed to the image of Christ. My hope, moving forward, is that your conviction might grow and that the Lord's influence in and through your life might abound. May you continue growing in your love for Jesus, striving to know Him more, and bringing others alongside you to encourage them along their respective journeys as well.

The thought of making disciples may be intimidating to you. If so, that's normal. But fear should never dictate how we live. What Christ accomplished on the cross and in the resurrection gained a victory that conquers all things, including your fear. And I hope this book helped you overcome some of those fears by wrapping your mind around a path that you can follow. Furthermore, I hope as you have now read through this book over the last several months, you are more equipped to study Scripture, more inclined to trust the goodness and promises of God, more emboldened to share your faith, more dependent on God's Spirit in your life, more involved in your church, more broken over the lostness of the world, more passionate about reaching the nations, more eager to present your request to God, and more confident of the riches that are yours in Christ.

May the rest of your life be marked by an ever-increasing love for God, an ever-increasing dependence on God's Spirit to move in and through your life, an ever-increasing effectiveness for making more disciples, an ever-increasing thankfulness for His daily grace, and an ever-increasing conviction to live a life worthy of the gospel—a life that accurately reflects the infinite, invaluable worth of Jesus our King. Then, and only then, are you truly living the Christ-centered life.

PART 5

EXTRA RESOURCES

FIVE QUESTIONS TO HELP YOU STUDY THE BIBLE

In John 15:7, Jesus told His disciples to let God's Word abide in them. To let God's Word abide in you means you allow His Word not only to guide you but also to govern your life. It means you see God's Word for what it truly is—divine authority. It means you view God's Word as the foundation on which you build your life values, principles, and goals. It means you approach God's Word as the source of salvation (John 6:63), sanctification (John 17:17), transformation (Romans 12:2), renewal (Ephesians 4:22–24), and revitalization (Ezekiel 37:4). You allow God's Word to search you and reveal all that is unholy (Psalms 139:23). It means you view God's Word as living and active, able to penetrate to the deepest parts of your soul and birth life (Hebrews 4:12).

Bible study is more than an exercise for gaining knowledge, although that is an important aspect of it. Study the Bible so you can know, love, and serve God better by applying His truth to everyday life (Ezra 7:10). When you allow God's Word to abide in you, God is glorified and your joy will be complete (John 15:8, 11). As you grow in knowledge and obedience to God's Word, you will find yourself growing more and more into the image of Christ, as the glory of God is revealed. Whether you are studying a whole book, chapter, paragraph, or verse, here are five questions that will help you study the Bible. These five questions are easy to memorize and follow the sequence: Context, God, Man, Cross, and Response.

1. What is the context of this passage?

The purpose of this question is to discern any related matter that will help you best understand the context in which the book or letter was written. There are two categories of context: the local context of the time and the context of the book. To discern the local context, you can ask questions such as:

- Who was the author and what was his relationship to the recipients?
- Why did the author write this book or letter?
- Were there any specific circumstances the author was addressing?
- What were the religious views and cultural practices of the recipients, and how would this affect the lens through which they viewed this writing?

To discern the context of the book, you can ask questions such as:

- What is the central theme of this writing?
- What recurring themes should I pay attention to?
- What is the thought process of the writer from the beginning to the end, and how does this passage fit within that structure?

2. What does this passage teach me about God?

The purpose of this question is to discern how God is revealing Himself in His Word, either as Father, Son, or Spirit. You can ask questions such as:

- Does this passage teach me anything about the character or will of God?
- Does this passage contain any commands I need to obey?
- Does this passage contain any promises from God that can provide me with hope?
- How should this passage increase my faith in God?
- What does this passage teach me about the glory of God?

3. What does this passage teach me about man?

The purpose of this question is to discern how God expects mankind to live. You can ask questions such as:

- Does this passage teach me anything about God's desire for mankind?
- Does this passage identify any sins I need to repent of?
- What does this passage teach me about believers and nonbelievers?

4. How does this passage point to the cross?

The purpose of this question is to see how all of Scripture (Old and New Testament) points to Jesus. The glory of God in the gospel of Jesus Christ is the central theme of Scripture. This means every passage will point to the cross of Christ in some way. You can ask yourself questions such as:

- How does this point to the cross?
- Because of the cross, how should this passage affect or shape my life?

5. How does God expect me to respond?

This question will help you make application of the passage. You should seek to apply God's truth by asking how this passage is relevant today and how it should affect your mind, heart, and actions. To do this, you can ask questions such as:

- Does this passage contain any godly examples I should follow?
- How should the truth of this passage affect how I think, feel, and act?
- Do I have any beliefs that contradict what I just read?
- Do I have any feelings, emotions, or affections that contradict what I just read?
- Do I have any behavioral actions that contradict what I just read?
- Does this passage teach me anything about how I can better reflect Christ?
- How does this passage teach me to reflect the glory of God in my life?
- How do I rely on God's strength to faithfully respond today?

NEW TESTAMENT
READING PLAN

The reading plan below will provide a path that will allow you to read the New Testament in three months. Studying both the Old and New Testament are important, but it is okay to start with the New Testament. There is not a requirement for how much or how fast one should read God's Word. In fact, if you read too fast to process what God's Word is saying and how it applies to your life, you are going too fast. So speed is not what is important; understanding and applying biblical truths are what is important.

It is no problem if it takes you longer than three months, as long as you are routinely meeting God in His Word. Schedule a time in your day you can set aside for time with God. You can refer back to my letters on Bible Study, Prayer, and Worship, as well as the Bible study questions I have included to help you get the most out of this time. You can use a highlighter or pen to mark things in your Bible you find interesting or difficult to understand. It may also be helpful to write your thoughts in a private journal so you can remember what the Lord is teaching you over time. Use the schedule to read on your own, but find another believer you can meet routinely with to discuss what you both are learning. This practice will be mutually encouraging and will help you understand even more. Bible reading is not just for growing in knowledge, though. It should lead your heart to worship as the glory of the Lord is revealed on each page (2 Corinthian 3:18). The Lord is near. Seek Him, and He will be found. Please be assured of my prayers for you as you study God's Word and grow in your relationship with Christ.

Day 1	Matthew 1–3	Day 23	Luke 19–21
Day 2	Matthew 4–6	Day 24	Luke 22–24
Day 3	Matthew 7–9	Day 25	John 1–3
Day 4	Matthew 10–12	Day 26	John 4–6
Day 5	Matthew 13–15	Day 27	John 7–9
Day 6	Matthew 16–18	Day 28	John 10–12
Day 7	Matthew 19–21	Day 29	John 13–15
Day 8	Matthew 22–24	Day 30	John 16–18
Day 9	Matthew 25–26	Day 31	John 19–21
Day 10	Matthew 27–28	Day 32	Acts 1–3
Day 11	Mark 1–3	Day 33	Acts 4–6
Day 12	Mark 4–6	Day 34	Acts 7–9
Day 13	Mark 7–9	Day 35	Acts 10–12
Day 14	Mark 10–12	Day 36	Acts 13–15
Day 15	Mark 13–15	Day 37	Acts 16–18
Day 16	Mark 16–18	Day 38	Acts 19–21
Day 17	Luke 1–3	Day 39	Acts 22–24
Day 18	Luke 4–6	Day 40	Acts 25–26
Day 19	Luke 7–9	Day 41	Acts 27–28
Day 20	Luke 10–12	Day 42	Romans 1–3
Day 21	Luke 13–15	Day 43	Romans 4–6
Day 22	Luke 16–18	Day 44	Romans 7–9

Day 45	Romans 10–12		Day 73	2 Timothy 3–4
Day 46	Romans 13–14		Day 74	Titus 1–3
Day 47	Romans 15–16		Day 75	Philemon 1
Day 48	1 Corinthians 1–3		Day 76	Hebrews 1–3
Day 49	1 Corinthians 4–6		Day 77	Hebrews 4–6
Day 50	1 Corinthians 7–9		Day 78	Hebrews 7–9
Day 51	1 Corinthians 10–12		Day 79	Hebrews 10–11
Day 52	1 Corinthians 13–14		Day 80	Hebrews 12–13
Day 53	1 Corinthians 15–16		Day 81	James 1–3
Day 54	2 Corinthians 1–3		Day 82	James 4–5
Day 55	2 Corinthians 4–6		Day 83	1 Peter 1–3
Day 56	2 Corinthians 7–9		Day 84	1 Peter 4–5
Day 57	2 Corinthians 10–11		Day 85	2 Peter 1–3
Day 58	2 Corinthians 12–13		Day 86	1 John 1–3
Day 59	Galatians 1–3		Day 87	1 John 4–5
Day 60	Galatians 4–6		Day 88	2 John 1–Jude 1
Day 61	Ephesians 1–3		Day 89	Revelation 1–3
Day 62	Ephesians 4–6		Day 90	Revelation 4–6
Day 63	Philippians 1–3		Day 91	Revelation 7–9
Day 64	Philippians 4–6		Day 92	Revelation 10–12
Day 65	Colossians 1–2		Day 93	Revelation 13–15
Day 66	Colossians 3–4		Day 94	Revelation 16–18
Day 67	1 Thessalonians 1–3		Day 95	Revelation 19–20
Day 68	1 Thessalonians 4–5		Day 96	Revelation 21–22
Day 69	2 Thessalonians 1–3			
Day 70	1 Timothy 1–3			
Day 71	1 Timothy 4–6			
Day 72	2 Timothy 1–2			

PRAYERS FROM THE BIBLE

It is sometimes difficult to know what to pray. The Bible provides many examples of prayers that can help you. Here are a few examples to help you get started.

"How long, O Lord? Will you forget me forever? How long will you hide your face from me? How long must I take counsel in my soul and have sorrow in my heart all the day? How long shall my enemy be exalted over me? Consider and answer me, O Lord my God; light up my eyes, lest I sleep the sleep of death, lest my enemy say, 'I have prevailed over him,' lest my foes rejoice because I am shaken. But I have trusted in your steadfast love; my heart shall rejoice in your salvation. I will sing to the Lord, because he has dealt bountifully with me." (Psalm 13)

"Now therefore, O our God, listen to the prayer of your servant and to his pleas for mercy, and for your own sake, O Lord, make your face to shine upon your sanctuary, which is desolate. O my God, incline your ear and hear. Open your eyes and see our desolations, and the city that is called by your name. For we do not present our pleas before you because of our righteousness, but because of your great mercy. O Lord, hear; O Lord, forgive. O Lord, pay attention and act. Delay not, for your own sake,

O my God, because your city and your people are called by your name."
(Daniel 9:17–19)

"Pray then like this: 'Our Father in heaven, hallowed be your name.
Your kingdom come, your will be done, on earth as it is in heaven. Give us
this day our daily bread, and forgive us our debts, as we also have forgiven
our debtors. And lead us not into temptation, but deliver us from evil.'"
(Matthew 6:9–13)

"I do not cease to give thanks for you, remembering you in my prayers,
that the God of our Lord Jesus Christ, the Father of glory, may give you a
spirit of wisdom and of revelation in the knowledge of him, having the eyes
of your hearts enlightened, that you may know what is the hope to which
he has called you, what are the riches of his glorious inheritance in the
saints, and what is the immeasurable greatness of his power toward us who
believe, according to the working of his great might." (Ephesians 1:16–19)

"I thank my God in all my remembrance of you, always in every prayer
of mine for you all making my prayer with joy, because of your partnership
in the gospel from the first day until now. And it is my prayer that your
love may abound more and more, with knowledge and all discernment, so
that you may approve what is excellent, and so be pure and blameless for
the day of Christ, filled with the fruit of righteousness that comes through
Jesus Christ, to the glory and praise of God." (Philippians 1:3–5, 9–11)

"And so, from the day we heard, we have not ceased to pray for you,
asking that you may be filled with the knowledge of his will in all spiritual
wisdom and understanding, so as to walk in a manner worthy of the Lord,

fully pleasing to him, bearing fruit in every good work and increasing in the knowledge of God. May you be strengthened with all power, according to his glorious might, for all endurance and patience with joy, giving thanks to the Father, who has qualified you to share in the inheritance of the saints in light." (Colossians 1:9–12)

"We give thanks to God always for all of you, constantly mentioning you in our prayers, remembering before our God and Father your work of faith and labor of love and steadfastness of hope in our Lord Jesus Christ." (1 Thessalonians 1:2–3)

"To this end we always pray for you, that our God may make you worthy of his calling and may fulfill every resolve for good and every work of faith by his power, that the name of our Lord Jesus may be glorified in you, and you in him, according to the grace of our God and the Lord Jesus Christ." (2 Thessalonians 1:11–12)

"I thank my God always when I remember you in my prayers, because I hear of your love and of the faith that you have toward the Lord Jesus and all the saints, and I pray that the sharing of your faith may become effective for the full knowledge of every good thing that is in us for the sake of Christ." (Philemon 1:4–6)

EIGHT POST-MEETING EVALUATION QUESTIONS

I have found from my own personal experience that it doesn't take me long after a discipleship meeting to agonize over whether or not the meeting actually accomplished anything. Only the Holy Spirit can regenerate the heart of man and cause God's people to grow, but the Great Commission calls each of us to help another learn to obey all Christ commanded. So evaluating how we are doing along the way is an important element of the discipleship process. We are all busy, and we need to make the most of every opportunity. So to help me evaluate a discipleship meeting, I wrote a list of questions to help me. These eight questions are not set in stone, and they are constantly being tweaked. Some are originally mine, while others have been borrowed from others much wiser than I. Hopefully you will find them helpful, but feel free to tweak, remove, add, or blow up the list and start over if that is best for you. It is important to point out that I don't discuss these questions with a person I am discipling. You could, but each letter already has questions specifically tailored for that topic. These eight questions serve to help me, the disciple-maker, evaluate whether or not I lead the conversation in a direction that was Christ-centered and applicable for Spirit-empowered transformation.

1. Was each participant prepared to discuss the questions?

2. Was Christ undeniably the center of the conversation?

3. Did each participant have a clear understanding of how the gospel shapes that topic to be centered in Christ?

4. Did each participant understand how that topic relates to the mind, heart, and actions?

5. Was the balance between personal responsibility and the power of the Spirit harmoniously applied?

6. Did each person leave the meeting encouraged by the hope of the gospel or discouraged for some other reason?

7. Did each participant leave with a measurable plan to apply what he or she learned?

8. What would I keep the same or do differently next meeting?

ACKNOWLEDGEMENTS

Discipleship is never accomplished outside good community, and neither is good writing. I am forever indebted to a tremendous community of colleagues and mentors who took the time to invest in my life and provide helpful feedback for this project. S. Ellis, B. Sullivan, Scott G., Jon and Shawna Cardona, Andy M., Jerry H., Matt J., J. Collins, T. Samplaski, R. Wallace, W. Brown, and H. K. Miller, your respective contributions added significant value to this work.

I want to thank my five closest national partners whose names, unfortunately, I am unable to list. You guys have taught me what it truly means to be a follower of Christ. I'm grateful for your patience as I butchered your language and inadvertently offended your culture. You've seen me at my worst, walked with me through difficult times, and rejoiced with me as mercies were renewed. I admire your commitment to the Scriptures and your passion to name Christ where He has not been named. Thanks for allowing me to walk this journey with you.

I want to thank my former missions professor from Southern seminary, Dr. George H. Martin, who challenged me to not just reach the nations but also to teach them how to obey deep theological truths through the instruction of personal letters.

I want to thank my home church, Highview Baptist Church, and the

IMB for your support and partnership in the gospel.

I want to thank Rainer Publishing and my editor, Christi McGuire, for your help getting this book in print.

I want to thank my friend, Andrew George, who patiently endured as I repeatedly asked about design and formatting. Your passion for and modeling of gospel-centered community is an inspiration to me.

I want to thank the Summer 6: Aly F., Gretchen Larson, Molly Grummer, and especially Marco D.R. Rivera, Adam Woelber, and Brianna Hovde for working tirelessly with me to revamp, tweak, delete, and rewrite pieces of this material over your summer break. It's amazing how long train rides and non air-conditioned fast-food restaurants cultivate creative synergy, all of which we now know well.

I want to especially thank M2B2, Mackenzie McLain and Brittany (Bartow) Doolittle, for your diligent service to critique, edit, format, design, and offer helpful suggestions from start to finish. You challenged me to be a better leader, and in so doing, a more devoted follower of Christ.

And to my wife, Taryn, thank you for your constant encouragement, patience, and invaluable contributions to this project. Your beautiful heart and dedicated spirit is a constant reminder that we serve at the pleasure of our King and to the praise of His glory. It took more hours to write these letters than I expected and more drafts than I care to mention, but I had the strength to persevere knowing your commitment to the cause was unwavering.

And finally I want to thank my friend and mentor, Dr. Chuck Lawless, for the countless hours you selflessly gave to this project. You recently reminded me you gave your time because you care for me as a person, but what makes that immensely more meaningful is your overt, genuine love for Christ and His church, which so clearly drives you. It is an under-statement to say this work would never have been accomplished without your continual coaching and assistance, reflected in the hours of editing and encouragement you gave through Skype calls and e-mails. My wife often tells me the best way to thank you is by giving my time and efforts to others the same way you so generously give those things to clueless guys like me. And, Lord willing, I will, because you showed me how.

INDEX

F

faith, 10, 13, 22, 25, 39, 40, 75, 80, 93, 101, 102, 105, 106, 107, 108, 109, 110, 111, 112, 113, 119, 123, 124, 130, 136, 149, 169, 175, 179, 180, 181, 186, 187, 192, 218, 225, 231, 239

faithfulness, 108, 110, 194

fasting, 63, 66, 67

final judgment, 204, 205, 206, 209, 210, 211, 212, 214

flesh, 51, 94, 99, 119, 125, 167, 204

forgiveness, 62, 107, 131, 142, 146, 174, 175, 200

G

glorification, 186, 188

glorify, 31, 32, 34, 35, 36, 37, 64, 86, 87, 89, 136, 220

glory of God, 31, 32, 34, 69, 82, 95, 111, 113, 143, 149, 157, 158, 168, 188, 229, 231, 232

God the Father, 32, 44, 112, 124, 162, 179

God the Son, 124, 163

gospel, 9, 10, 13, 14, 16, 19, 20, 21, 22, 23, 26, 31, 32, 34, 35, 37, 38, 39, 40, 41, 42, 43, 47, 49, 50, 51, 52, 53, 56, 57, 59, 65, 69, 70, 71, 73, 74, 75, 76, 77, 78, 79, 80, 82, 83, 87, 88, 89, 93, 95, 97, 100, 101, 103, 109, 114, 115, 117, 120, 121, 124, 125, 126, 127, 131, 132, 133, 135, 136, 138, 139, 141, 144, 145, 147, 148, 149, 150, 151, 155, 158, 159, 165, 168, 169, 170, 171, 173, 175, 177, 183, 189, 192, 193, 195, 201, 207, 209, 210, 213, 217, 218, 219, 223, 224, 225, 231, 238, 242, 244

grace, 20, 27, 31, 39, 55, 74, 80, 88, 107, 111, 112, 113, 119, 125, 131, 137, 149, 162, 163, 170, 173, 174, 175, 176, 179, 181, 185, 200, 203, 211, 220, 223, 225, 239

Great Commission, 9, 10, 13, 15, 16, 39, 80, 136, 149, 212, 218, 241

L

M

N

O

P

partnership, 147, 148, 151, 152, 238, 244

pastor, 33, 193

Paul, 3, 32, 34, 37, 38, 69, 74, 75, 87, 94, 99, 101, 113, 124, 125, 142, 143, 148, 155, 157, 175, 179, 192, 203, 204, 218, 219, 220

peace, 20, 62, 107, 111, 113, 126, 129, 130, 131, 132, 133, 134, 135, 219, 220

persecution, 124, 125

perseverance, 129, 186

Peter, 13, 56, 74, 82, 86, 112, 117, 119, 156, 162, 163, 174, 180, 186, 191, 192, 198, 205, 235

prayer, 3, 16, 55, 58, 60, 61, 62, 63, 64, 65, 66, 67, 76, 137, 147, 148, 150, 156, 193, 237, 238

R

reconciliation, 73, 134, 138, 142

regeneration, 181

repentance, 50, 176, 181

resurrection, 38, 69, 70, 80, 81, 112, 114, 158, 163, 173, 176, 225

return of Christ, 20, 107, 206, 209, 210, 212, 214

righteousness, 51, 55, 107, 113, 130, 155, 157, 163, 174, 186, 203, 211, 237, 238

S

salvation, 21, 27, 44, 80, 86, 107, 114, 174, 175, 176, 178, 179, 180, 182, 183, 185, 188, 189, 229, 237

sanctification, 46, 49, 50, 186, 229

Satan, 125, 168, 200, 203, 205, 206, 208

saving faith, 75, 181

Scripture, 2, 9, 11, 16, 25, 50, 51, 57, 58, 62, 80, 95, 96, 100, 101, 113, 119, 136, 143, 149, 155, 156, 157, 158, 162, 193, 198, 205, 210, 225, 231

NOTES

1   John Piper, "Can Joy Increase Forever?" *DesiringGod.org*, May 5, 1998, http://www.desiringgod.org/articles/can-joy-increase-forever.

2   John Piper, *God is the Gospel: Meditations on God's Love as the Gift of Himself.* (Wheaton: Crossway, 2005), 42.

3   John Piper, "God Is Most Glorified in Us When We Are Most Satisfied in Him," *DesiringGod.org*, October 13, 2012, http://www.desiringgod.org/messages/god-is-most-glorified-in-us-when-we-are-most-satisfied-in-him.

4   The Southern Baptist Convention, "The Baptist Faith and Message," accessed June 17, 2016, http://www.sbc.net/bfm2000/bfm2000.asp.

5   John Piper, "Love One Another with Tender Affection." *DesiringGod.org*, June 4, 1995, http://www.desiringgod.org/messages/love-one-another-with-tender-affection.

6   John Piper, "The Fruit of Hope: Joy," *DesiringGod.org*, July 6, 1986, http://www.desiringgod.org/messages/the-fruit-of-hope-joy.

7   The Southern Baptist Convention, "The Baptist Faith and Message," accessed August 1, 2013, http://www.sbc.net/bfm2000/bfm2000.asp.

8   Wayne Grudem, *Bible Doctrine: Essential Teaching of the Christian Faith* (Grand Rapids: Zondervan, 1999), 296.

9   Ibid., 288-290.

10 Ibid., 302.

11 Ibid., 288.

12 Ibid., 315-319.

13 The Southern Baptist Convention, "The Baptist Faith and Message," accessed August 1, 2013, http://www.sbc.net/bfm2000/bfm2000.asp.

14 Ibid.

15 Grudem, *Bible Doctrine*, 200.

16 The Southern Baptist Convention, "The Baptist Faith and Message," accessed August 1, 2013, http://www.sbc.net/bfm2000/bfm2000.asp.

17 Ibid.

18 Grudem, *Bible Doctrine*, 348–360.

19 Grudem, *Bible Doctrine*, 348–360.

20 Grudem, *Bible Doctrine*, 453–455.

92345423R00154

Made in the USA
Lexington, KY
02 July 2018